White Man... in a Black Man's World

*Learning to be Black
While Wearing White Skin*

Richard Vermillion

Copyright © 2002 by Richard Vermillion

White Man...in a Black Man's World
by Richard Vermillion

Printed in the United States of America

Library of Congress Control Number: 2002111319
ISBN 1-591602-34-3

All rights reserved. No part of this publication may be reproduced or transmitted in any form or by any means without written permission of the publisher.

Unless otherwise indicated, Bible quotations are taken from the Authorized King James Version.

Xulon Press
11350 Random Hills Road
Suite 800
Fairfax, VA 22030
(703) 279-6511
XulonPress.com

To order additional copies, call 1-866-909-BOOK (2665).

Dedication

Without a doubt, *White Man In A Black Man's World* needed to be dedicated to my parents who taught me to judge others by the content of their character and not the color of their skin. Thank you for raising me in a home free from racial discrimination so that I could acknowledge people from every tribe and color for who they really are. Donna and I love you very much!

Acknowledgments

The first person I need to thank is my Lord and Savior, Jesus Christ, who has truly enabled me to become a "white man in a black man's world". Without Him, I would neither have such a testimony to share, nor would I have been able to accomplish such a task as writing this book. Thank you Lord! You are truthfully my ultimate best-friend, *who sticks closer than a brother*!

I must also give my love and show my appreciation for my wife and best friend on Earth, Donna. She labored with me in this project mightily, and without her love, support and efforts, this book could never be what it is. *Thank you my sweet*! You are so precious in my eyes.

Thanks needs to be shared also with my son, "J.R.", who had to be without Daddy more than he would have liked while I pushed forward with this project. *Thank you son for being such a blessing to your momma and me*! We love you!

Finally, I wish to thank all our friends and supporters, who have encouraged us, helped us, prayed for us, and in some cases, financially blessed us. *You have been so instrumental in keeping us going*. Thank you for your love!

Contact Information

Richard Vermillion would love to hear from you concerning how White Man In A Black Man's World: Learning to Be Black While Wearing White Skin has impacted your life. If you would like to contact the author, you may write him at:

Richard Vermillion
P.O. Box 29266
Richmond, VA 23242

Please specify also if you would like to be added to his mailing list, and include your e-mail address if you wish to correspond with him via the Internet.

If you would like to inquire about obtaining Richard Vermillion for speaking engagements or media appearances, please contact:

Harvest International
PO Box 472287
Aurora, CO 80047-2287
1-800-607-0073
www.his-harvest.com
Email: hi@his-harvest.com

Introduction

My story seems to be one that is different than most, at least that is what people keep telling me. I have shared parts of my story with a few friends, family, and acquaintances, and I kept getting the same reactions: "Wow! I've never heard anything like that before," or, "You need to write a book!" So here I am! Doing just that: writing a book to share my story and the lessons learned through the experiences I've encountered along the road of life.

The providence of God has moved me from one scene to another in a drama that has played out through my entire life. His guiding hand has been orchestrating the events that have shaped my destiny and formed my character.

This book is a reflection of that drama and the lessons learned. It is the story of my own personal struggles as I face the issues of race, culture…and racism.

I have been to places you may have never gone, and seen things that you might have never seen. Through my struggles and pains, you may be able to feel what you may have never felt, and experience perhaps what you have not experienced.

Come with me and peek behind the curtain of races you may have not known to see things you may have never been aware were there. Let me show you the thoughts, attitudes, and paradigms of people whose skin color may be different from yours, and whose culture to whom you may not relate or perhaps even understand. My desire is that you would gain greater empathy and comprehension for another race that will lead you to peace and reconciliation within *yourself*; that bitterness would disappear, hatred would be turned into love, and segregation and distrust would become acceptance and harmony. Oh, I'm sure you will read things that are not new to you, but perhaps you might see them in a different light.

White Man in a Black Man's World is my testimony about what I've learned concerning race and culture in general—American black and white folks specifically—but, more importantly, it is about God's love for **all** mankind. And, perhaps by examining **ourselves** a little closer, we will also begin to understand others more clearly.

Contents

Dedication v
Acknowledgments vii
Contact Information ix
Introduction xi
Chapter 1   My Friend Tony 15
Chapter 2   Culture Shock 23
Chapter 3   Middle-School Mayhem 35
Chapter 4   Abandon Ship! 41
Chapter 5   Back to Black 53
Chapter 6   Heading West 63
Chapter 7   Bridging the "Sensitivity Divide" 71
Chapter 8   Political Racism 77
Chapter 9   Teaching Mike? 87
Chapter 10 Dark Red or Light? 103
Chapter 11 White Man in a Black Man's…Church? 109
Endnotes 117
Bibliography 119

CHAPTER 1

My Friend Tony

I grew up initially in a suburb of Richmond, Virginia, just barely inside of Henrico County, near Brian Park. It was not a wealthy neighborhood at all. The homes were mostly brick, dating back from the construction boom following the Second World War—cape cods and a few two-story homes mostly, with a few other styles scattered here and there among them.

My parents rented a small two-bedroom "cape" a couple of blocks from the park. They were just getting started in life, fresh out of the military and raising a small kid. I was a few months past my first birthday, I suppose, when they moved there. Therefore, that is the first house I remember.

The neighborhood was white upper-lower class to lower-middle class. A few true "middle-classers" were scattered here and there in some of the larger houses. All my friends were other kids in the neighborhood, so they were all white by ethnic origin. We did all the normal kid stuff, like ride bicycles, climb trees, and play games. We all went to the same elementary school, and we rode on the same bus to get there. The school we attended, Lakeside Elementary, at that time was basically composed almost entirely of white children from lower to middle class families; basically we were a whole bunch of white kids, growing up in a white culture, attending a predominately—almost exclusively—white school.

There was at least one kid in our school, however, who was an exception—his name was Tony. He was the only black kid I know of that attended our school while I was there. I do remember seeing one other African American child, a girl, who was probably in about the second grade when I was in the forth. However, before that, there was just Tony.

I remember initially meeting him in first grade. He was a great kid! I really did not care that his skin color was darker than mine or that his hair was an afro. Who cares about such things when you are five or six? None of the other kids in our class cared either, as far as I recall. We were just kids! We learned our lessons, took naps on little blue mats at naptime, ate lunch and snacks while comparing lunch boxes, and *lived* for recess. That was all that mattered to us. Who cared about the external differences? Nobody.

Tony was just like us—if you overlooked his tan. He talked like us, played like us, and was just a kid as we were. In fact, he and I were friends. I think that perhaps the color of his skin and the texture of his hair kind of made him special to us, in a way. After all, most of the kids had never really been around any black people before, not in a social setting like school or something. He was *unique*, and his uniqueness made him special. I'm sure we did things like touch his hair or feel his skin. There was nothing "racially motivated" about that desire except to satisfy our curiosity. He was different *physically*, and that made him interesting to us at first. However, the novelty soon wore off and we got over it as we became used to seeing him in class. Furthermore, he acted just like we did anyway. So "who cares what he looks like?"

Kids do not have a racist bone in their body at that age, unless it is put into them by an adult. They will adopt somebody different from themselves in a moment, and the next thing you know, they are all outside playing kickball. You are accepted in their eyes. Love comes naturally to them. Hate has to be *learned*. Children pick up racism from their parents and other adults. It is a *learned behavior*, not a natural one, especially for a child.

I remember meeting two racially bigoted children once out on the playground one day. (Brothers, I think.) And I could not believe the words they were using to describe black people! Only intentional indoctrination into bigotry by their family could have trained these two white kids to be so hateful toward another race. I recently drove through the neighborhood surrounding that elementary school just to recollect my experiences there and found it still predominately white. One house was actually proudly flying a Confederate flag on a pole in the front yard! To be sure, most of the people in that community are not so extreme, but I imagine that these two kids came from a similarly racist home back then. Children are not racist from the womb, they are *trained* to be that way by family, culture… and occasionally experiences.

My father and mother were not in the least bit racist, so there was no bigotry to learn from them at home. I did not have a parent telling me, "Don't play with that n——r!" to sow seeds of discrimination and intolerance into my heart. No, on the contrary, my parents tried to protect me from racist seeds of hate and misunderstanding.

Mississippi Mud

There is a story I remember that my mother and father told me about that took place when we had moved down to Mississippi for the summer when I was about seven. My parents were investigating the employment situation down there to consider whether to move to that state. Dad's mother lived in a particular town of Mississippi on the Gulf coast, so Mom and I lived with her while Dad returned

White Man...in a Black Man's World

to Richmond and worked the job he already had up there. My mother found employment as a nurse in one of the local hospitals. My grandmother also kept herself busy with a volunteer position of some sort at the same hospital.

Because everybody was working, my parents had to find someone to watch me while everyone was away. Before my father returned to Richmond, he, my mother and grandmother took me to the house of some woman my grandmother knew to arrange for this individual to baby-sit me while they were all occupied. This person was about a decade younger than my grandmother and was taking care of some other children in her home. Essentially, she ran an in-home day care. In fact, she had actually watched over my uncle, Charles, when he was about my size—roughly fifteen or twenty years prior to then.

My parents told me later in life that upon our arrival, this "lady" had started into some very vulgar racist chatter about some issue or another she was watching on the television. "Those n———rs! They're ruining this community! Those n———rs even robbed a filling station yesterday! It was on the news this morning!" Grandma apparently just jumped right in and participated with her in this bigoted vulgarity.

My father was enraged and said something in the vein of, "I don't appreciate your racist garbage, nor do I want such filthy trash spoken around my son!" He went on to rebuke my grandmother for participating in such a dialogue and made it clear that he did *not* want it around me at all.

Grandma, and this other woman, apparently felt ashamed and tried to defend their ignorance and bigoted language by saying "It was how we were raised!"

Dad pointed toward all the children playing on the floor (including me) and said something akin to, "So why are you doing it to them? Why perpetuate the bigotry? Why don't you just stop the intolerance now?" He told me when I was older that, knowing he was not going to be around all summer, he wanted to "set the tone" before his departure to ensure his son would not be subjected to all that racist propaganda while I was in Mississippi.

I do not remember that woman, or Grandma, ever saying racial vulgarity again in my presence after that—excluding a few "slips of the tongue" when they were not attentive to themselves. In any case, my parents decided not to move to Mississippi, and my father returned at the end of the summer to retrieve his family and we drove back to Richmond.

I thank God that we didn't move down there, given that racism is far more pronounced in that part of the country than it is in Richmond, Virginia. God's providence had changed our course in this situation for, although I have nothing against Mississippi, it was not part of my *destiny* to be raised in an atmosphere of racial hostility, as it existed back then. God's plan for my life **required** I learn to accept people of other races and cultures, not discard them for their ethnicity.

> *Before I formed thee in the belly I knew thee; and before thou camest forth out of the womb I sanctified thee, and I ordained thee a prophet unto the nations.*
>
> (Jeremiah 1:5)

Just like Jeremiah in the Old Testament, God had a plan for my life before He formed me in the womb—a plan which He would reveal to me sometime *after* I had accepted His Son as my Savior. In the mean time, however, He certainly was orchestrating my paths and preparing me for my future.

Furthermore, I also believe it was the providence of God that I was not raised up north, in the Pittsburgh, Pennsylvania area, for example, where my mother's side of the family was from. I would find it so curious growing up that whenever we visited up there around the Christmas holidays, I would hear racial slurs among white people in that northern region. I can remember hearing more racist comments in a week of conversations between my older relatives up there than what I had heard down in the "South" the whole previous year! I thought it strange that I had to go up north to hear the "n——r" word so much.

Later, as an adult, I found out that racism is quite prominent in various areas of the "North." In fact, a pastor friend of mine in Beaver, Pennsylvania, told me that western Pennsylvania has the largest population of Ku Klux Klan per capita outside of the state of Georgia! Therefore, you do not have to go "south" to find ignorance of race and culture.

I am very thankful that Jesus was directing my paths to fulfill my destiny because things could have easily turned out differently.

Where's Tony?

Despite all the potential influences that could have led me toward bigotry, I was able to remain pure in my heart toward people of another color—as *every* child should. I just enjoyed my buddy Tony as we enjoyed our childhood together at that predominately white elementary school. We were growing up together in childlike innocence. However, after we completed the first grade, I soon found myself without my darker-skinned friend.

Tony went somewhere else to school after that year. I did not know at the time if his family had moved or what had happened to them. All I knew was that, I looked for him, but my friend did not return the following year. That saddened me. Kids will be kids, however, and it did not take me long to get over it and just live for the moment. Children can be that way, you know. Upset one moment about something, then easily distracted to the events of the next. I did think about him from time to time, however, and wished

My Friend Tony

he were still around. "Oh well, no matter. Who's going to pitch the kickball at recess today?" Children are funny about things like that.

A few years went by...second grade passed...then third...and suddenly, Tony reappears! By the forth grade my friend had returned. I was quite excited to see him in my class that first day of school. He was about a foot or so taller and a few pounds heavier, but so were the rest of us. We had a grand time hanging out together in class and did most things together all day. He was my buddy again. I think that perhaps having missed him the previous two school years created for me an extra close bond to him in this forth grade.

All my life I have been drawn to black people. They have always seemed to get my attention and attract my curiosity. In fact, I am generally drawn to people of other races and cultures. It seems I cannot get enough "diversity" to satisfy my "curiosity" of other people and their ways. This even includes different "white" ethnic cultures like Irish, and Italian. It is so good to be open-minded! You can learn a lot from others as a result, for the reason that no one people or group "has it all". Diversity makes life interesting and helps us to grow, individually and as a community.

Again, there were no noticeable differences between Tony and me that I can remember, except his tan was a whole lot darker than mine was. Oh, then there was the hair also. It was still about a three- to four-inch afro, as I can recollect. But, who cares? He was just another kid, and the differences just made him unique. We talked the same, played the same—we were just alike on the *inside* in terms of culture and mindset, just different on the *outside* in appearance.

Fortunately, it also seemed that I did not have any racist teachers that I know of. They did not appear to mind Tony being in their classes, or the fact that all the white children were playing with him freely...and openly. I believe that this too was God's providence.

The school year seemed to fly by, and the next thing we knew, summer break was back again. I did not see Tony the following year at Lakeside Elementary when we returned for the fifth grade. I figured that perhaps they had moved again or something. Again, I was disappointed, but my own life was beginning to take on a whole lot of changes. Those rather distracted me from the thoughts of missing my friend Tony, although I did wonder where he had disappeared to.

During Christmas break of my fifth grade year, my parents closed on their first house. It was not elaborate, but it was their *own* house, bless God! (There is just something about home *ownership*.) It was a nice two-story brick colonial on a corner of Brook Road in Richmond City. We only moved about a mile from our previous house near Brian Park, but we were in the **city** now... not the county. Different area, and, of course, different schools. While other children were focusing on Christmas presents, family and food, I was off to another house and another school...or was it another world?

CHAPTER 2

Culture Shock

We moved into our new house in Richmond City and tried to settle in. A couple of weeks during the holidays is not much time to get unpacked and fully settled, but we managed. January rolled around and the time came to attend my first day at my new school, **Ginter Park Elementary.** Mom drove me over there for my initial visit and escorted me to my new class.

"Whoa! What is this? I have never seen a school like this!" (Not that I had ever seen any other schools.) It sure was different! The school building dated back to something like the year 1905, so its architecture and facilities were quite…unique. However, there was another difference I noticed about that school which really caught my attention: about seventy percent of the other kids looked like **Tony** did—black skin and kinky afros! On top of that, almost all of the teachers looked like Tony also. (Except quite a bit larger, of course.) All the teachers at Lakeside were white (back then), so my exposure to African American adults had also been non-existent until that moment.

I was quite nervous my first day, as you can imagine. Not only was I going to a new school where I did not know anybody, but now

White Man...in a Black Man's World

I was a minority myself! Perhaps not as much of one as Tony had been at Lakeside, but a minority nonetheless!

The teacher welcomed me into the classroom the first day and introduced the new student to the class. "Children, this is our new classmate." She seemed excited I was there. The other white kids seemed excited too, as if they were thinking "Wow! Another white kid! We're increasing!" Whereas the black children varied in their interest from one to another.

I started trying to assimilate into my new school environment. However, since I had never been in a new school before, it was disquieting just trying to learn all the new names. I had grown up with all the children I attended Lakeside with, so names were not an issue. Here, though, I had to learn everybody's name. To make matters worse, most were significantly different from what I was used to in the Caucasian culture: Lawanda, Deshawn, Laticia...I had never heard anybody named like that before. "Could you say your name again?" I asked time and time again, trying to figure out what in the world they were saying. "What ever happened to the simple names?" I thought. " How about Bob? Or, David? Or, George?" Those names seemed few and far between at times.

Furthermore, there were other differences. There was a distinct difference in how *these* black kids talked and acted verses what I had been accustomed to with my other school's classmates—and even Tony. You see, Tony was raised around white folks, so he acted like we did. ***Culturally speaking***, he was the same as we were by all appearances. But not these kids. Most of them were growing up in almost completely African American neighborhoods and apartment projects (subsidized housing for low-income families) with very few white children around their homes. Since the black children were isolated from much contact with whites, they were growing up primarily in a culture totally different from the one in which I had been raised until that point.

As I mentioned before, this often meant that they talked differently. In fact, compared to that to which I was accustomed, it was almost another language. They would say things like, "Yo man! Wassup?"

"Huh?" was my first reaction. The dialect also was so different that, even if the language was the one I understood, I often could not get what they were saying the first time or two they tried. Some of them probably thought I was hard of hearing for all the times I had to have them repeat things. Communication problems were the first issue I began to be challenged with as I tried to "fit in" in my new environment, but not the only one.

The next obstacle I had was that of comprehending how they dealt with *confrontation*. In the school I had been in before, if you had a problem with another kid (another boy, that is) you both just simply "duked it out" while the other kids stood around and cheered you on! This would last until one of you ran away, gave up, or a teacher arrived on the scene. It was a very effective way of settling disputes, so I thought, and I was able to hold my own. Consequently, I got along pretty well in my elementary school social circle...until Ginter Park, that is.

These kids settled disputes quite differently! First of all, there were a couple of girls in my class who were substantially bigger than I was! I am not sure if they "blossomed" early, or if they had been held back a grade or two. Whatever the case, I was not used to that at all—especially when one of them beat me up in a fair fight! (I hate to admit it, but it is true.)

Second, the boys were likely to fight as a *group* against you if you did not watch yourself. I was quite surprised one day when I was suddenly defending myself from a gang of third-graders in the restroom!

Finally, they did not fight *fair* (at least by the rules I was used to). I would confidently square off to give them a few good licks, only to wind up scrawling on the floor holding my...well...you know what I mean. It is one thing to be whipped in a fair fight; it is quite another thing to get a surprise kick down *there*! That was something that we just ***never ever*** did at my other school!

The ethnic lessons were only beginning, though. Remember the communication problems I mentioned earlier? They got worse. I would notice that the black kids would call each other names that, up until then, I had thought were derogatory terms to use. "You n——r," they would say to each other, and then laugh about it. Well, I wanted to fit in so I tried joking around with them by saying, "Hey, n——r!" It did not go over very well...Nope! Not at all!

Then there were phrases that we used all the time at my other school between each other, but *these* kids seemed to get upset about it. At Lakeside, for example, children would call out "Hey, boy!" to another kid whose name they did not know, trying to get their attention. We commonly communicated that way all the time at my other school—"hey, boy," or "hey, girl." But when I tried it at *this* school, "Hey, boy!" ...

"**Who are you calling <u>boy</u>?**" they would angrily snap back. Shockingly, they got quite heated about that one.

"What's going on with these kids?" I thought to myself. "Why are they getting so upset with me over calling a kid 'boy'? He didn't *look* like a girl..." I just did not get it.

Then there was "Tom". I heard a couple of them calling each other "Tom" in the hall while laughing together one day, so I figured that they both had the same name. "Hey, Tom!" I said to one of them later when I saw him.

"*I ain't no Tom!*" he yelled back. You would think he would have corrected the other kid also if his name was not "Tom". Again, I just did not get it. I figured out I had just better change the way I addressed the kids I was unfamiliar with if I wanted to avoid a fight.

A white kid growing up exclusively around other white kids is in for a real culture shock when he finds himself the minority in a predominately black school. I began to figure out that the other white kids at this school seemed to have things figured out already concerning these things. They were accustomed to exposure to the African American culture and had already figured out many of the racial taboos, so I tried to hang around them and learn a bit.

The school year ended finally and, thank God, I had survived. "Sixth grade will be much better than fifth was. After all, I'll be going over to a brand new middle school instead of this old building," I thought to myself.

A Little Help for My Caucasian Reader...

My African American readers are probably thinking about now, "Wow! Where was your brain? Why didn't you know to avoid saying those things?" Well, my answer to you is another question: *where would I have **learned** to refrain from saying them*? It is obvious that my Caucasian ethnic origin and its culture did not prepare me in the least bit for what I was encountering. Why? *Because the Caucasians I grew up around had not learned about it either—* particularly children.

In fact, I realize that a whole lot of my Caucasian readers are probably just as clueless as I was about many of these same terms and racial taboos. For that reason, I think this would be a great time to take a moment and help you white folks "catch up" with the rest of us so I do not leave you behind wondering, "What was the point he was trying to make anyway?"

Let me explain the three names or labels that I was challenged with in the above story: the "n——r" word, "boy", and "Tom". The "n——r" word is that very divisive and offensive word that white bigots frequently use to describe blacks. Not "Negro". That word is simply one derived from the Spanish word, "negro," which was derived from the Latin word, "niger" (one "g"), all of which simply mean the color "black". No, I am talking about that other word…you know the one I am talking about. The "n———r" word (the one with two "g's".)

"Why don't you just write it out?" you might ask. Because I find the word offensive. It is a mean and ugly word that just reeks with the stench of racism and bigotry, and I refuse to have it in my vocabulary. Its origin was in hate, and it's continued existence supported by malice.

"Why then were *they* calling each other by that term if it is such a bad word to begin with?" one might ask. I have no idea. I did not then, and I still do not today. You see, there seems to be in many people a peculiar characteristic that says, "You can call me a derogatory name *if you are like me*. If you are *different* than me, then I am offended." A person of a particular ethnic origin, gender or social group can call a person of the same classification by a derogatory term applying to them both, and they'll often times both laugh about it. By the same token, if a black person calls another black person a "n———r", it's all a big joke! However, it is **not** a joke. It is not any more proper for an African American to refer to his own race or another person as a "n———r" than it is when a foul-mouthed white person does.

I have actually felt just as uncomfortable and "unclean" after hearing a "n———r" joke told by a black person, as I have when I have heard one told by a white bigot. I do not permit anybody to tell me such vulgarity directly, although I cannot help what I hear in a public setting sometimes.

For my African American reader, let me challenge you with this thought: Jesus said, in effect, "you have whatever you say," in Mark 11:23 of the Bible, and Solomon said, "you are snared by the words of your mouth," in Proverbs 6:2. So, if you want to be limited by that "n———r" label, just keep letting yourself and other black people call you that.

If, however, you want to rise above that label in life and above its racist heritage, do not ever allow another black person to label you by that derogatory term again. Neither should you ever use that word as a description of yourself (or another) any longer. I have rarely heard a self-respecting and ambitious black person refer to themselves or another so crudely. You need to have more respect for yourself if you want to ever become all God has ordained you to be.

I am not saying you should be rude or abusive toward other black folks if they do use that word toward you. I just encourage you to correct them lovingly and say, "I don't identify by that term any longer. I have more self-respect than that. I am simply, an African American. Thank you," or whichever expression you prefer to use to describe yourself. Since "n——r" has such an evil and abusive origin, it should be considered "foul language" today, no matter who is using it... or the color of their skin.

Back to my "Caucasian Assistance"...

The term "boy" was used by white slave owners and racist whites during the entire two hundred years of slavery in the United States as a demeaning way of addressing a Negro. Its use continued as a derogatory "put-down" when addressing an African American after the Civil War had ended by embittered whites bigots, and its use continued throughout the Twentieth Century. Unfortunately, it is still used by bigots today. Consequently, it is *understandably* offensive to a black person to be called "boy" by a white person, whether the white person meant anything by it or not. Furthermore, like the "n——r" word, I'm of the opinion that it shouldn't be a term used between black folks either due to its equally foul origin (unless another definition or application of the word is meant by the context of the conversation, of course.)

Finally, we come to this "Tom" business. I am sure a whole lot of white folks have no idea about this one, because I know that I did not. While I do not claim to be an expert on black history, I have done (and continue to do) a little investigation through the years on this and related subjects, and so I will share with you what I have found. Perhaps it will encourage you to do some more exploration of these topics yourself.

"Tom", or more completely, "Uncle Tom", is the fictitious main character in a book entitled, *Uncle Tom's Cabin*, written by Harriet Beecher Stowe and published first in an abolitionist paper called the *National Era* as a series in about 1851, and later as a book in 1852.

Mrs. Stowe was a white abolitionist vigorously opposed to the institution of slavery due to her moral convictions as a devout Christian, and her contact with escaped slaves she assisted in Ohio, where she lived. Their stories of the atrocities they endured as slaves so moved her, that she chronicled many of them in this anti-slavery novel. In so doing, she personalized the plight of the American slaves in a single person the reader could relate to and sympathize with, a slave named "Uncle Tom" as well as others.

Uncle Tom was a devout Christian, as well as a slave. The book's panorama covers many events, people, and the brutal abuses of slavery—but it is Tom's selfless acts of love and Christian devotion that are some of the most moving. After being sold to a monster of a slave owner, a Mr. Simon Legree, Tom even wanted to see his newest and cruelest slave master saved—despite the man's contempt for Tom's Christianity. He endured great tribulation at this man's hands while praying for his salvation, and was eventually tortured to death by him. Readers of the day were so moved by the character's Christian love and the atrocities of slavery as they were chronicled in Mrs. Stowe's novel, that they became *enraged* against slavery, especially in the Northern states, fanning the flames of the already growing abolitionist movement.

The book sold an astounding 500,000 copies in five years in the United States alone, which would be an astounding feat even for today, much less in the 1800's. Considered by many the catalyst that drove the anti-slavery fervor in America, this book caused the abolitionist movement, and the Republican Party, to expand rapidly in the Northern portions of the United States. This movement led to the election in 1860 of the newly formed Republican Party's presidential candidate, Abraham Lincoln, and to the beginning of the Civil War. Lincoln himself credited her book with these events when he first met her saying, "So you're the little woman who wrote the book that started this great war." [1]

Many do not realize that the Republican Party itself was *founded* on an Abolitionist platform to end slavery, and Abraham Lincoln as President did just that—in part with the *Emancipation Proclamation*, and later by pushing the 13th Amendment to the Constitution through the Republican-controlled Congress and necessary state ratification. All this can be attributed to the providence of God (who Himself opposes slavery) and in part to His use of this one book, *Uncle Tom's Cabin*.

"Well, if this fictional man 'Uncle Tom' was of such noble Christian character that this book was a catalyst for such positive change on behalf of blacks in this country, why do they consider it an insult to be called an 'Uncle Tom' or 'Tom'?" Good question. Here is the answer: ***slander***.

"Slander?"

Yep.

"Of whom?"

The Reverend Dr. Martin Luther King, Jr...

Probably the greatest single figure of the Civil Rights Movement of the 1950's and 1960's was a bold Christian black man by the name of Dr. Martin Luther King, Jr.. His bold, yet biblically righteous stand against segregation and Civil Rights abuses committed against African Americans captured the attention of the world and even won him a Nobel Peace Prize. His method was one of non-violent protest, and his speeches captured the attention of the whole country, and the world.

People all over the United States and the world were moved to sympathize with the Civil Rights movement as they saw peaceful black protesters being knocked down with water hoses by hostile white firemen and gassed aggressively by white police. They were mesmerized by his eloquent televised speeches that communicated the righteousness of his cause with simple truth, profound phrases like "I have a dream," and references to Scripture and Gospel hymns. The effectiveness of Dr. King's non-violent Christian approach was evident in dramatic shift of public opinion to side with the Civil Rights cause and the subsequent laws passed on the federal level to abolish legalized segregation and enforce the Civil Rights of minorities.

However, not every black person agreed with his methods. In the 1960's, splinter groups cropped up trying to address Civil Rights issues through violence and advocating other aggressive means that Dr. King was directly opposed to. One of those other groups was the Black Muslims, and one of their most prominent spokespersons was a man named "Malcolm-X". This man referred derogatorily to Dr. King as "Uncle Tom" in reference to the similarities of Christian conduct and character that was evident between this fictitious character and Dr. King himself. Malcolm-X, and others like him, considered Dr. King "weak" for his biblical approach to the Civil Rights Movement, and likened him to the selfless character "Tom" of Mrs. Stowe's novel who suffered greatly at the hand of white men while professing the faith he believed.

Like many people who do not know Christ, Malcolm-X did not know the *power* of the Gospel nor the truth in Dr. King's speeches. He did not realize that Dr. King's "meekness" was actually *power under control*, and Dr. King showed much greater strength to endure abuse and imprisonment *without* "lashing back" than others were by advocating such impulses. It takes a strong person with self-control to stand boldly in the face of oppression and injustice, and speak "the truth in love" for the purpose of **changing** the other person rather than to hurt or destroy him. This was Jesus' approach, and so it was also with Dr. King.

Later in his life, and before his assassination, Malcolm-X began to understand where Dr. King was coming from and began to amend his own philosophy and approach to Civil Rights. However, because Malcolm-X had already initiated the use of "Uncle Tom" as a derogatory label, the damage had already been done. "Uncle Tom" (or its shorter form, "Tom") came to be associated with a weak black man who let white people walk all over him, rather than its *original* 100-plus year meaning of strong Christian character in the face of abuse and injustices. I do not know about you, (and I realize that I am white,) but I would not mind at all being compared to Dr. King by being called a "Tom". In terms of his public work as a Civil Rights leader, he is the finest example of an African American activist I know, and a model to be emulated by people of all races, color, and creed. Though his private life had some issues that were not biblically sound and undermined his cause to some, his **public** character and conduct in dealing with Civil Rights abuses reminds me of Jesus Christ Himself.

No, it would not bother me at all to be called "Uncle Tom." I would be in good company; but then again, I am not black.

I hope that for my Caucasian readers, that helps to explain a few things and change your "paradigm" because of a new level of understanding in these issues. Perhaps it may have even done the same thing for my African American readers in the process.

Anyway, back to my story...

CHAPTER 3

Middle-School Mayhem

Henderson Middle School was almost new and I was quite impressed with the facility on my first day. Summer had been nice and I was looking forward to a much more successful school experience. The experience was wonderful in my new school with respect to my new teachers. I had great favor with them, and I also developed great favor with the administrative staff. They even had me make announcements over the intercom every morning! Pretty cool stuff for a twelve-year old.

However, though my experience with the teachers and staff had been upgraded a notch or two, the social problems became worse. Much worse. Really, a whole lot worse. **I mean bad!** (Get my point?) Many of the same kids I had problems with in the previous school came over to this one, and it seemed they had spread the word about me. Due to my ignorance of the black culture that I had suddenly found myself immersed in, I had developed a reputation with a few of the kids as a "racist", even though I really hardly knew what the word meant at the time.

This "racist" label seemed to get much worse at the new middle school—not with *all* the black kids, however. Most of them were

White Man...in a Black Man's World

quite nice and realized I had no animosity toward them. This was especially true of the ones who were in school *to learn something*. I had several good friends among this group of black students. I did not have such problems with the teachers, either. No, they thought quite highly of me because I was respectful and a quick learner.

The problem was with a relatively small percentage of the kids, but "OH! What a problem!" It was with the kids who really did not want to be in school at all. The ones who cut class, smoked cigarettes in the bathrooms, and would kick their feet up on the desks in class and joke around while the poor teacher tried to do her job. They had no respect for authority, and even less for me. You know... the *"hood"*.

Most of them were older than me, and much bigger. Some were probably supposed to be in the eighth grade or more (others at least seventh) but had failed a time or two. They were quite ignorant scholastically because they did not *want* to learn anything, just "be cool". That was their thing—being "cool". If theft was "cool", they would steal. If cutting class were "cool", they would cut class. Moreover, if beating up on the "million dollar white boy" was "cool", then...beat up on me they did!

That was one of the nicknames they gave me—"million dollar white boy." They got that nickname from my last name, Ver**million**. "Million dollar white boy" was only one of the racial tags they gave me, however. Their favorite was "KKK" (after, of course, the Ku Klux Klan—a white supremacist group of notorious reputation). Not exactly a fun label for a white kid, *especially when attending a predominately black school*!

Oh, they also tried the various regular slanders (whitey, honky, etc...). None were very pleasant names to call anybody white, especially a kid. I had been labeled by them as a racist, even though I had not really shown any *true* evidence of being one. I was getting along fine with other black kids and teachers. So why brand me a "racist"? Ignorance! That's why! Theirs...and **mine**.

My Ignorance

My ignorance of the black social customs and cultural taboos put me in a position to offend many of them. Ignorantly, of course. Let me add one more word to that also... *innocently*. How can anyone expect somebody of another race or culture to understand their own if that person had never been exposed to it or taught? Really, they cannot. But, actually, *they do.*

White people used to expect black people to act a certain way at one time in this country. In some places, they still do. Whether the culture is Oriental, Native American, Hispanic, or whatever, if someone comes into their social climate uninformed, it is quite easy for that person to step on some toes. Violation of social and cultural taboos can be quite a divisive thing...and sometimes get the offender in much trouble.

Sometimes, the offended can become *violent*. They did with me. Labeled a white racist, I became the target of a great deal of "reverse discrimination". That's the *technical term*. Realistically, it is called *hate*. In my case, it was often called "brutality".

Their Ignorance

Not realizing that the remarks that were offending them were simply ignorant comments from an ethnically uneducated kid, they interpreted my bad judgment, and slips of the tongue, as "racism." Innocent mistakes, *mistakenly understood*, can lead to racial strife.

They were responsible for their own actions, but one could not really blame them only. What else could be expected of them? Some within their culture told them all or most white folks are "racist" anyway. "The system will always try to put you down," they are often told. "The white man is your worst enemy. Don't trust him!"

White Man...in a Black Man's World

Really, it is a rehash of the propaganda of the violent splinter groups of the Civil Rights Movement back in the 1960's, such as the Black Muslims and Black Panthers (some of these groups still exist today). Although most African Americans are not necessarily advocating violence, certain elements within their culture are still telling them they are "under oppression"... ignoring the many advances their race has made in this country. Please remember this: as long as you are oppressed in your *mentality*, you will be oppressed in your *reality*, because most of the time, *you* determine your own world. You can either change it, or leave it the same—the choice is yours. Jesus came to set you free, so why are you still sitting behind open prison doors? It is time to walk out!

Well, their bad information did not mix well with my lack of it. In addition to the daily intimidations and threats, I was beat up at the lockers, ganged up against in the restroom, and suffered other violent acts.

On one occasion, about a dozen of them attacked me after school on my way walking home. I determined to try to fight them off. I figured, "If I could put up a good fight, they might leave me alone." Wrong! It did not deter them at all! After one of them kicked me in the back, I decided to fake paralysis. "My legs! My legs! I cannot move them!" I know it really sounds silly, but it actually worked!

After they took a quick look in my book bag for valuables, finding only textbooks, they left me alone. As soon as they had gone around the corner, I jumped up and took off running for the house! **(Fear can really get you *movin'*!)**

Fear. That is what it is all about really, is it not? Afraid of another race or culture.

I cannot say that I have ever experienced legalized segregation. Nobody ever told me I had to drink from a certain fountain, use a certain restroom, or go to the back of the bus. No. I cannot empathize with the degradation that the older African Americans of this country have had to endure when racism was public policy in America. I respect those who have, and honor them for their endurance and patience under such oppression. I also rejoice with them that God has helped them and destroyed that evil system of apartheid that existed in this country, as well as in others around the world, although in some places it still does exist.[2]

I can say, however, that I do know what it is like to be made to fear for my life and safety because of the color of my skin. I can also say I have experienced violence that was racially motivated. I have been called racial slurs and have had great hate directed toward me, all due to the color of my skin and the culture I came from. It may have been ***reverse* discrimination**, a frustrated response to *perceived* racial prejudices, or perhaps reactions to past offenses from others, but it was still hate. It was still discrimination. It was nonetheless, **racism**.

I may have been misunderstood by them, but it still hurt—inside and out. It may have been all a "big mistake", but I was still the victim. They may have had what they *perceived* to be a justification for their actions against me, but it was still wrong. A twelve-year-old kid is not in a position to consider all the cultural and historical significance of the cruelty he endures. He is just plain scared. The psychological pain was just as real as the physical, and honestly...I just could not take it anymore. Something had to change.

CHAPTER 4

Abandon Ship!

My parents had been getting a steadily increasing flow of information from me about the suffering that I was experiencing. It started out as an occasional comment, but toward the end of the school year, they could tell I was getting desperate. They did not really understand what I was going through, mainly due to my inability to communicate the matter effectively. The embarrassment and emotional pain I was suffering caused me to internalize much of my suffering and so they did not grasp the scope of it all.

They knew I was getting into fights (or rather—getting beat up!), but did not comprehend the racial hate directed toward me. How could they? They had never experience anything like it, and I was not very good at communicating it to them at the age of twelve. It was, however, becoming increasingly obvious I was scared—really, panicked over it!

The following year I was enrolled in a small private school. They were able to find one that was not outrageously priced, and with a few financial adjustments, they were able to swing it.

Bitterness

I will admit that I had some resentment as a result of the previous school year. It is hard for someone to go through what I had without Jesus in their heart and come out without some bitterness.

Yes, I will go so far as to say that it was racial bitterness. I was quite indignant concerning how some black youth had treated me.

Although I knew that many of my black school-mates had been quite friendly toward me, I still had some anger. Not toward all African Americans mind you, but enough to be suspicious of most.

I can see how people from other races and cultures can develop suspicion, and even **hatred**, towards another ethnic group, if members of that group had oppressed them at some point in their past.

They do not *have* to, but I can understand how they *could*.

Apart from Christ and a true heart-based relationship with Him, anybody can get bitter toward another race or group of people.

Labor against management. Male against female. Black against white. Gentile against Jew. Sinner against Saint. The atrocities that we endure can be used by the enemy to instill bitterness, resentment and hate in all of us.

The enemy? Yes, I am talking about the devil, Satan.

He is the enemy of our souls, and the origin of all that is evil and destructive.

He will influence others to offend us, and then turn that same offense into an opportunity to implant bitterness into our souls. "Did you see what they did to you? How they looked at you? Are you going to let them treat you that way?"

The funny thing is that much of the time, they are innocent errors by others...but magnified through our hurts, they become great offenses.

(I guess it is not so funny after all.)

Of course, there *are* the times that the offenses are real.

"Get to the back of the bus!"
"Who let *you* in here?"
"Million-dollar white boy!"
Whatever the words, the hate is quite real.

Violence, persecution, malicious words, whatever the form of the offense, sometimes it is quite real and not just a matter of perception.

The question still remains: will we allow other people to poison *our* lives with *their* hate and ignorance?

One minister has said "When they spoke their bigotry, it was *their* problem. When you internalized their remarks and got offended, it became *your* problem."

You can choose to be bitter, or you can choose to forgive.

You can choose to take offense, or you can choose to leave offense where it already is...with them.

One statement that has really affected me in my adult life came from a Jew who had survived a Nazi concentration camp. In essence he said, "I have one right nobody can take away from me, and that is the right to choose my own attitude."

He chose a good one.

He chose forgiveness.

No wonder he was a survivor.

Another Jewish man once said, "I have been beaten, cussed at, spat upon, and called all kinds of names...but I have *never* been *offended*."

Wow! If we could all rise to that level, this world would be a better place.

Although I did not measure up to such a high standard at that point in my life, I was not nearly as bitter as I could have been. After all, I realized that it was partly my fault in how I presented myself to those I was around.

Additionally, I had many African American classmates that I

got along with just fine.

Yet still, there was some bitterness for a while...but obviously, I got over it.

When will you?

Going Private

My new school was Luther Memorial, a small but quite nice private school a few miles further into town from our home and still within the city limits. It was small, virtually all white, but nice.

I was starting there in the seventh grade.

The educational standards were much better than the public school I had attended. One homeroom per grade (K-8), so it was pretty small in comparison to Henderson Middle.

There was no more racial tension for me to have to deal with—at least not any directed toward me, that is.

There were still a few interesting racial lessons to learn there, however.

Being in an almost all-white environment (there was only one black girl in our class, the rest were in lower grades than ours) opens up the door for a whole lot of ethnic insensitivity, stereotypes and, of course, "n——r jokes."

White kids telling other white kids jokes about a race they know little to nothing about...jokes they probably picked up from their relatives at home.

This is not unusual. Get a group together that exclusively of one race, in the absence of cross-racial sensitivity, and you will get jokes about other races slipping into the conversations here and there.

"How many [blank] does it take to screw in a light bulb?"

"There were three men in a boat: one Jewish, one Irish, and a [blank]..." (Usually the terms were not very nice, so we will just omit them here for sensitivity's sake.)

Nothing unusual. No harm really done...most of the time. Just some harmless humor...right? However, I noticed something there. Something strange that was stirring inside of me. Something that I did not expect to happen, particularly after all that I had just been through the previous school year. I was becoming somewhat offended.

"What?" you might ask. "Offended?"

Yep.

"But you were white!"

I still am (according to skin color anyway).

I know... it seems crazy, doesn't it? I could not understand it at the time either.

I am not saying I was offended in the way some persons might be. I was not violent about it, or resentful. What I mean is that, on the inside of me, I could hear myself saying, "You don't know anything about black people. Who are you to make fun of a race you don't know anything about?"

At Henderson I had learned pretty well how to talk ethnically "black", and even walk like they walked (by necessity, of course.)

I was trying to overcome the communication barriers and social misunderstandings that had caused me so much torment. I had to survive as a minority in the midst of a black majority. I was trying to understand the African American mindset to the point that I could at least not step on any more toes.

However, in the process I had also somehow picked up a certain empathy for African Americans. Somehow, an understanding of how African American people felt about racial matters had "seeped" into my thinking—to a point, of course.

By innocent ignorance and error, I had repeatedly crossed over into sensitive areas of racial tensions that had been **bred** into my black classmates by their parents and culture.

It had caused me much pain personally as they responded in hurt and anger to my intrusion by lashing back.

Reverse discrimination had hurt me physically and emotionally, *but it had also **taught** me*.

It taught me that certain terminology, coming from a white person, was offensive and hurtful to an African American person. I did not really understand *why*... that was to come later. However, I did learn not to say "hey boy" to a black guy.

I did not really understand (yet) the reasons for their racial sensitivity. But I knew they were often *very* sensitive.

These youth at Luther Memorial, had themselves never had the benefit of having been around African Americans much at all, *and they were ignorant.*

Ignorant of black culture. Ignorant of racial issues. Ignorant of *race*, if you want to really get down to it.

For the first time, I understood how I must have looked to the black students when I first arrived in their environment.

I could see my own initial ignorance in these "white" kids. Somehow, I was looking at them as though it were from a black person's perspective. I actually felt like a minority again because I was identifying with my black classmates from my previous school and I could not understand it.

I began to really see, for the first time, how utterly ignorant most white folks are concerning racial issues.

What many non-white people do not understand about white folks in America is this: ***they are not ethnically conscious.***

What does that mean?

Let me explain.

American "Mutts"

First, "white" is not really a race or ethnic identity in and of itself. There are people who have tried to make it one, but I will discuss them in a minute.

Italian...Irish...Scottish...English...German...French...Russian....

Abandon Ship!

these are cultural and ethnic identities. "White" just happens to be the color of their skin, for the most part.

Now, if a person says, "I'm Italian," then they are identifying with an ethnic origin. If they say "I'm Irish," that is identifying with an ethnic origin. However, if the person says, "I am white," they are either just telling you the color of their skin, or, really, they are subconsciously saying, "I don't have an ethnic origin that I can identify with."

You see, most "white" folks in the United States are descended from a variety of cultural backgrounds.

Take myself for example: I have ancestors that are French (hence, the last name Vermillion), German, English, Scottish, Cherokee Indian, and another Native American ancestry, which we think may be Navaho Indian. In other words, I'm a "mutt" genetically.

I cannot, according to the flesh, really identify myself ethnically.

I could, perhaps, pick one of the ethnic backgrounds, like German, for example, and try to identify with it. The problem is that I was not raised in a German home or around German culture. Therefore, I would have to *learn* an ethnic culture to adopt one. (Cultures can be learned, by the way; it is done all the time.)

The American "white" man and woman are in just such an "ethnic limbo".

Unless the person can look back to their parents or grandparents who may have come over to this country in a recent generation, they really cannot identify culturally to an ethnic origin.

Now, there are some white folks who have tried to make "white" a race in and of itself. These people are "white supremacists" and are, basically, bigots.

In a way, they are white folks trying to establish their own ethnic identity. The problem is, they are often doing so on a foundation of hate and malice toward all other races... particularly African

Americans and Jews. Some even try to claim a racial *supremacy* over other races—this is simply ignorance multiplied by pride.

These people are not the "norm" in white American culture, to be sure. In fact, most white folks really think such people need their heads examined. Anybody who exalts his or her own race over that of another (particularly if they really do not have an ethnic 'race' to begin with) is simply ignorant of how God created this whole thing to start with.

There are areas in parts of this country that were predominately settled by Italians, Irish, or whatever. Those areas are ones in which the people still have a consciousness of their original ethnic identity, but they also are a minority among "white" Americans. Most of us are just simply "mutts". The only culture we know is the American culture as a whole, which is really a mix of dozens of other cultures, primarily from Europe. Therefore, simply saying one is "white" is really saying, "I don't have an ethnic identity, as such." Their only identity ethnically is, for all intents and purposes, "American".

"American" has really become an ethnic identity in and of itself amongst the white folks. "It's as American as apple pie!" is an example of American ethnicity in a phrase. They view oriental people, middle-eastern people and of course black folks as "different" when they express their ethnic identity in ways that differ from the "norm" of American white culture. The fact that they look different is, of course, an issue to some degree or another, but more often than not, it is the *cultural differences* that make it harder for the "mutts" to relate to such people. (If you act like a white person culturally, they will usually accept, and in some cases not even notice, your ethnic origin after a while because they can relate to you.)

How they talk, what they wear, how they act. These can all be sources of misunderstanding...and on a few occasions, hostility or discrimination. People tend to fear what they do not understand, and what people fear, they will try to avoid, destroy or distance themselves from.

> *There is no fear in love; but perfect love casteth out fear: because fear hath torment. He that feareth is not made perfect in love.*
> *We love him, because he first loved us.*
> *If a man say, I love God, and hateth his brother, he is a liar: for he that loveth not his brother whom he hath seen, how can he love God whom he hath not seen?*
> *And this commandment have we from him, That he who loveth God love his brother also.*
> (1John 4:18-21)

This leads us to the next issue: ***ethnic ignorance***. Ethnic ignorance in the American "white" population is the result of primarily two conditions: a lack of an ethnic identity and living as such as the majority "race" of the population. Since the majority population of the United States is (by skin color) white, and most of them do not have any real ethnic identity themselves (other than "American"), then they really do not understand anybody else's ethnic identity either. Nor have they historically had any real motivation to even try to understand the concept of ethnicity, much less actually learn to appreciate another race. Therein lies part of the source of the racial problems for the minorities in America. *People without cultural ethnic identity cannot understand someone who has one.*

This is a weakness in human nature that tends to divide people and spread hate. All they know is "they're unlike what I'm used to." Often times, this perception of difference becomes a basis for hostility or discrimination. Moreover, since they are in the majority, they do not perceive a **need** to understand minorities or to change their own behavior. Really, this happens around the world wherever a minority ethnic group is present within a majority culture. It seems to be a "universal" problem. Racial discrimination can be found in every country of the world.

We have all seen in the news where a majority population oppresses or afflicts the minority one. This is often the case in "developing" nations as well as many Middle-Eastern and Asian countries. In some cases, especially in Europe, it is only an extreme element of the population, which perpetuates these crimes. Regardless, however, the situation is the same—the majority population does not understand, nor is it sensitive to the needs of the minority and sees them as "foreigners". In many cases, they are actually hostile toward them and problems arise as a result.

Here in America, the "white" American culture does not for the most part teach its children ethnic sensitivity or understanding. That is why, as a fifth-grade kid, I walked right into an ethnically oriented school and stepped on a whole bunch of toes there. Here I was at this private school seeing numerous other white youth doing the same thing. Fortunately, they had enough sense to keep these things to themselves when there were minorities around.

In addition, let me add that it really was not out of any hostility toward minorities that they were acting that way, simply ignorance and insensitivity. One reason why I can say that is because an African American girl was in our class and was accepted as "one of the kids" by the rest of her classmates. To my knowledge, she never experienced any hostility or true bigotry directed toward her, and like I said, they had enough sensitivity not to say those things in her presence. They were just ethnically ignorant, like most white Americans are.

Despite their innocent ignorance, however, I was still learning. Providence was continuing to work secretly in my life, teaching me some very important lessons, and He was not yet finished with my education either. There was still very much more to learn...

CHAPTER 5

Back to Black

I attended Luther Memorial for my seventh and eighth grades. Since the school only went as far as the eighth, I relocated to a different private school my freshman year of high school. Unfortunately, that school completely closed at the end of my freshman year and would not be opening for the next. My parents were at a quandary as to where to send me my sophomore year. The remaining private schools were quite expensive—far more than the two I had just attended.

While they were deliberating on the subject, I was doing some introspection. I started to consider possibly going back to public school. I spent a few days of that summer break really analyzing my previous state of affairs. "Why was I experiencing so many problems getting along with those other kids at Ginter Park and Henderson Middle? Why did they hate me so much?" I realized that the circumstances had a whole lot to do with me as well as with the other children. "If I was consistently having problems with the black kids, perhaps there is something I can do to change how they view me," I thought to myself.

Obviously, as I discussed before, if the other kids had not been conditioned by their families and culture to be hostile toward *perceived* racial infractions, then I could have gotten along better as a result. A little bit of mercy and understanding on their part would have gone a long way to alleviate the situation. However, I realized that a great deal of the problem was in how I presented myself to them. I realized that there were other Caucasian kids in the school who were not having any problems with reverse discrimination akin to what I was (although, my problems were making a few of them nervous).

Many times, we have problems relating with other people, and we wonder what *their* problem is. Perhaps the problem is actually in us—how *we* are acting. While I am not denying that there can be true cases of racism and unjust discrimination, I am saying that we need to check-up on ourselves and see if perhaps many of these problems might just really be caused by *our* attitudes or character flaws. (Even when the bigotry is **real**, we can choose to keep a good attitude in the face of injustice and cruel behavior—just like that Jewish fellow I mentioned earlier.)

I have seen African American people over the years that walk around with the proverbial "chip on their shoulder" and wonder why they are always "discriminated" against. "Bunch of racists!" they think. "Won't give me a job because I'm black!" However, the reality is that they came to the interview late, and would not look the person in the eye, but rather, kept staring at the floor. They gave incoherent answers to the interviewer's questions and displayed an attitude like "you're not going to hire me anyway, because I'm black and you're white!"

Their own bad attitude *attracts* negative responses from other people and they blame it on racism, or gender, or whatever they can, to avoid dealing with the real issues within themselves. Many times, it is simply *our* **attitude**. We need to wake up! We all have flaws in our personalities that need to be worked out over time. We all need an attitude adjustment on occasion.

That is what I did that summer. It was a process that only took a few days. I simply meditated on the past events and conflicts to see what I had been doing wrong. Once I discovered the problem within my own character (specifically an issue of conduct) I *decided* to change. I decided to change the way I talked with people, acted toward them, and my whole approach to social interaction in general. All it took was a ***decision.***

Decisions are very powerful things. They are an exercise of one's own God-given will. He gave you and me the right to make decisions that will affect any and every aspect of our existence. You can decide to change and see your life improve, or decide to stay the same and keep the mess you presently have. A decision to change can improve a marriage, repair a broken relationship, open the door to promotions, and even decide one's own eternal destiny. Yes, Heaven or Hell, ***it is your decision.*** Jesus paid the ***price***, but you have to pick up the ***merchandise***. However, that is another sermon...

Back to my story....

My decision at that point in my life was to change. I re-evaluated the circumstances surrounding previous challenges I had undergone. I walked (in my mind) back through time...year by year, incident by incident, all the way back through the racial problems I had experienced. I considered my conduct, my ignorance of ethnic taboos and issues, how I reacted to various situations, and how others reacted towards me. It was at this point that things really began to come together in my mind. Understanding was really setting in.

Flashing through my mind was every incident, word, and confrontation–from my first *culture shock* experience, through the problems of the sixth grade, to the ignorance I perceived among the "white" kids in seventh and eighth. It all began to make sense to me somehow. It was all becoming quite clear.

The revelation excited me...the enlightenment challenged me...it *could* have been different...it *can* be different...it **will** be different! A new decision had been made. I left my room and went down stairs to my parents. "Mom, Dad? I have made a decision. You do not have to be concerned anymore about trying to come up with the money for me to attend another private school. I will go back to the Richmond public schools. Let me attend John Marshall." That was the high school for that area—*right next door to Henderson Middle*, where I had experienced most of my problems before. Naturally, it was predominately black as Henderson had been.

Shocked, they asked "Are you sure? You had such problems before, we do not want to see you go through those things again..." My mother was especially nervous about this suggestion.

"Those things will not happen again," I answered, "Things will be different this time."

After we discussed it further, they cautiously agreed to my decision. They were not too certain how this was going to work out for me to return to a predominately black school again. Nevertheless, they *were* relieved not to have to pay for it! Seeing my confidence and desiring a financial reprieve from the burden of private school, they sighed in relief, and said, "Alright, if that is your decision..."

That was only *part* of my decision. I had also decided how to conduct myself once I got there. I had a plan!

When In Rome...

First, I decided how *not* to behave. That is, to avoid stepping on the racial taboos I had previously discovered. Obviously, there could be no more "Tom" or "boy" references. I certainly had that one figure out!

Next, I decided that I would "buddy up" to the biggest, toughest, and most "respected" guys on the school campus. I figured that if I was their "buddy", *they* would not mess with me. In addition, anybody who would want to pick a fight with me would think twice about messing with these guys and their "buddy" Richard.

Finally, I decided to "infiltrate the culture".

"What in the world do you mean by that?" you might ask.

Well, as the saying goes, "if you can't lick-em, join-em"! I decided apply what I had learned about Afro-American dialect and culture and basically "when in Rome, do as the Romans do". I talked like they talked, walked like they walked (I added a little "hip-hop" stride to my step), and even learned a how to rap a little (that was just becoming the "thing" at that time). I even started clapping on the second and forth beat instead of the first and third, as most white folks do. (A little rhythm goes a long way toward cultural acceptance among the black folks, I found out.)

Basically, I applied the lessons I had learned to present myself to the other students in a manner that was both culturally sensitive as well as just simply something that they could identify with. If I could be their "White Tony" so to speak, then they would not take any issue with the color of my skin just like we did not take any issue with Tony's before.

Furthermore, I would not seem "odious" to them. I would not come across as "racist" to their perception as I had formerly done. I would be perceived *inclusively* instead of *exclusively*, acceptable instead of reject-able, and a racial *ally* instead of an enemy.

"Did it work?"

Yep! Exceptionally well, I might add.

Oh, I was still a brainy kid, making straight "A's" in biology and volunteering as the computer lab assistant. Somewhat of a "geek" intellectually (I still am, really), **but I was a *cool* geek!**

I was actually both accepted by the faculty with great favor (because of my intellectual ability) and the other students as well because, "Hey, Vermillion is pretty cool." I was "wise as a serpent, and harmless as a dove," as Jesus said in Matthew 10:16.

The question might also arise, "Did you see any of the kids you had problems with before and did *they* give you any trouble?" Actually, I did see most of them, but they apparently had matured quite a bit more and the three years of time that had elapsed had softened memories. A couple of them jokingly said, "Hey, weren't you the million-dollar white boy?" They seemed almost astounded at the difference in my demeanor. "Yeah," I replied with a smile, and walked away (just in case).

I do not mean to say that I was just "putting on" as far as trying to "act black" either. I did still maintain much of my "Caucasian" personality (after all, I was not raised in this culture—and we all need to be ourselves). I simply decided to assimilate into their culture, to an extent, by allowing many of their ways to become my ways. Really, it added a little "flavor" to my life. As one Caucasian some time ago said, "I'm not as 'white' as I used to be, but I'm not as 'black' as I *want* to be either!"

I was applying the lessons previously learned to my newest Afro-American public school experience—and it worked! I enjoyed a successful year my sophomore year there at John Marshall. God's providence was still working on my behalf! Moreover, the lessons I learned that year (through practical application of what I had discovered before) would influence me for the rest of my life.

History Lessons

The summer between my junior and sophomore years, my parents and I discussed moving to another area so that I could attend another school.

Despite the fact that I was getting along with the other students at the school, I still had trouble truly relating to most of the students heart to heart. I did not have any truly close friends, or for that matter any girlfriends (although interracial dating has never been a taboo in my thinking), so my social needs were not truly being met at that particular school. I had not yet discovered the secret ingredient to multi-racial and multi-cultural integration; and without that ingredient, it is very difficult to form heart to heart relationships with people who think differently than you do. That ingredient (being born-again through faith in Jesus Christ) I was to discover later in life, but at that time it was eluding me...and the lack of close relationships was difficult for me to bear.

I had actually become quite depressed over the whole social issue, so my parents figured it was time to find another house in another area so that my social interests would be better cared for. That summer we looked at houses in the suburbs all around the Richmond area, but were not successful in locating the right house, so back to John Marshall I went for the beginning of my junior year. I had a positive attitude, however, because I knew that a new house (and a new beginning) was in the works.

Naturally, one of the classes that I had to take when I returned to school was history. On the first day of class, I strolled into the room in time to hear my African American instructor announce, "The first semester of the new school year we will be studying the Civil War."

"Great!" I thought, "I love war history! Generals...battles...cannons...this is going to be wonderful!"

If he ever mentioned battles or generals at all that whole semester, he only did so briefly—in passing. Rather, he taught extensively on the Underground Railroad, slavery and the atrocities committed against the black men and women during that time of American history.

"Good" some of my black readers may say, "You *should* discover that side of history and learn how white men oppressed the black man!"

White Man...in a Black Man's World

I agree—whole-heartedly, in fact. However, you have to understand, that **I was the only "white" kid in the whole class!** It can become quite tense in the atmosphere when your black teacher tells you and all the black students around you what terrible things white people did to their ancestors. It made me a little nervous, to say the least. Remember, I had once had a few problems with reverse discrimination previously, and I did not want this guy to stir up any more!

I kept thinking, "When is he going to get off the slavery kick? He is making me pretty uneasy in here! I want to hear something about the generals or a battle or something. Anything but week after week of white folks messing with black folks! Give me a break!" I was beginning to get desperate for that move to the suburbs.

To be honest, it was very obvious that the teacher had a real passion for the subject matter being taught. His racial sensitivity (perhaps over-sensitivity) and bitterness permeated the tone of his teaching. Thinking back on it, I really do not think he expected to have a white kid in the class. He did seem somewhat surprised when I showed up on the first day, but that did not deter him from making sure these African American students were quite aware of their history of oppression.

"Shouldn't African American children be taught their history?"

Yes, they should, but *not* in such a way as to create a mindset of oppression and bitterness, for then they will have trouble rising above it...and rise above it they must. Along with the history of this country and its founding fathers in general, they should be taught the richness of their own ethnic history, culture and of those African Americans that have made a difference to black people, the nation and the world. If they are taught the *right* things about the *right* role models and history, then they will both know "where they've come from", but also where they *can go* if they will just go for it! They will have a "free" mentality, not an oppressed one. They will have a bright vision for the future, instead of a depressed one that leads them to hopelessness and despair. Every child, no matter what the color of his skin, has the potential within himself to change the world *if* that potential is cultivated instead of suppressed by negative indoctrination.

Well, let us get back to my story.

My history teacher never really did get off of the slavery subject the entire semester. No real discussion of the generals, only a mention or two of some battles, but lots and lots about African American oppression and slavery. It would not have been so discomforting if it had not been so racially bitter in the way it was taught.

I was surprised to learn a great deal of the information he was presenting, however. I did find much of the history of African Americans quite enlightening as to how their culture and the general mindset of many African Americans had been formed. It helped me to understand some of the behavior I had been exposed to within this culture and also the rhetoric many of the black leaders in America were propagating. The class was quite enlightening, howbeit also quite unnerving...almost daily. I was never so happy for a semester to end as when that one did! Whew!

My parents had located a house we were all happy with in the far west end of Henrico county, away from the city and its schools. We moved over Christmas break, just like we had done originally when we moved to Richmond in the first place, so I began my next semester in a new high school out in the suburbs.

One note, before we go into the next school, that I thought would be very interesting to you for me to mention: my homeroom teacher my junior year at John Marshall turned out to be the mother of my Lakeside Elementary School buddy, Tony! What a surprise when she and I figured out who we each were. Of all the people I could have had for a teacher and I ended up with Tony's mom! I found out at that time that they had been moving frequently, so that is why he would come and go from my first school. His mother was quite nice with an understanding and compassionate demeanor that made her a joy to have as a teacher. It was easy to see why he had been such a great kid. Tony and I never reunited in person since he was at another school, but his mother did communicate between us our welfare to one another on a few occasions. What a blessing!

Anyway, off to the county...

CHAPTER 6

Heading West

The Mills E. Godwin High School was of predominately white middle-class to upper-middle class composition. There were some black kids there—probably about 5% of the school population at that time I estimate. However, most of the African American students, if not all of them, had been raised in a predominately-white environment, and therefore the cultural differences were minor.

The other thing I noted about my new school was the difference in the quality of education between this school in the county and its city counterpart. I had been in "honors" English at John Marshall so my new counselor asked me the first day my parents and I arrived to enroll at school, "Do you want to be in honors English here?" I was not sure...something told me I might not want to. "Honors English or 'B' level English?" she asked again, noticing my perplexity. I did not know, so she suggested that she invite the honors English teacher down to the counselor's office to describe her class to me so that I could see if I was suited for it.

When she arrived, she began to describe what they did in that class. "We do one book report, write at least one paper on some topic, cover this and that, and so forth." On and on she went for about five to ten minutes, I guess, listing all the different things they do.

"Is that per month or semester or what?" I asked.

"Oh, that's all what we do in one *week*!" she answered.

Shocked, and without hesitation, I looked at the counselor and said, "I'll take 'B' English."

Wow! What a difference! After spending the semester in what they called "B" level English, I realized that it was equivalent to what the city schools were calling "honors" English, perhaps even a hair better. It really is a travesty—the low standards of the city schools, which are primarily composed of minorities, verses the county schools, which are primarily yuppie white folks (and a few yuppie black folks too).

An education is one of the foundational building blocks for good character and success in society. There should not be such a great difference in standards from one school district to another, in my opinion.

In fact, at the time of this writing, the most recent report I read on the schools in this part of the state of Virginia that revealed which districts passed the new national Standards Of Learning (SOL) was shocking. It showed that the county schools surrounding Richmond, including Henrico—where Mills Godwin was located, all had 55% or more of their schools passing the SOL's, while Richmond City schools had only 6% passing. The differences in educational quality have apparently advanced quite *insignificantly* over the years in the Richmond schools since I originally noticed the disparity years ago.

The next surprise came when I went to the first day of my new history class.

"We are going to study the Civil War this semester", my Caucasian teacher said.

Déjà vu!

"Oh, great," I thought, "I'm pretty burned out on this subject, thank you very much!"

However, instead of black oppression, the underground railroad, and slavery, we got battles...and generals...and cannons and such. Barely a mention about slavery, the *Emancipation Proclamation*, black oppression or any of those type of subjects.

At first, I was quite thrilled. "At last! Thank God! No more squirming in class!" But after a while, as the semester progressed, it seemed strange to me that this white lady teacher was teaching this white student class everything except what the war was really all about. Rather, she emphasized more so that "states rights" was the reason the South seceded from the Union and formed the Confederacy and thus began the Civil War. This is true, except that the "right" that the Southern states wanted to keep was the right to own and trade slaves! Black Americans and their rights as human beings was what it was really all about!

Oppression as a culture and state institution was **the issue** that inflamed the passions on both sides of the Mason-Dixon line and resulted in a war. Somehow, that was kind of overlooked...skimmed over at best, through the semester.

In the light of what I had learned the previous semester, this semester caused me to observe an important lesson in race relations and racial issues. **African Americans are oftentimes *over-sensitive* to racial issues due to an overabundance of emphasis being placed on them in their culture and education, whereas white folks are usually _insensitive_ to racial issues because of a *lack* of education on the subject.**

In the previous school, an overly sensitive and bitter teacher taught the black students, "You are an oppressed people...white folks have put you down in the past and have done you wrong, stole your heritage and denied your rights," while implying the whole time, "and they still are."

In this school, nothing...nada....zip! A white teacher saying *nothing* of the past mistreatment of African Americans (or the lessons learned) to a predominately white class. Oh, slavery was mentioned, in passing...however, not the Underground Railroad that I remember, and certainly neither of them was explained in detail or in the least bit emphasized.

Interestingly, I remember that Harriet Tubman's picture and biography in relation to the Underground Railroad *was* in our textbook...nevertheless, she was omitted *in class*. It marked me, because of what I had learned of the subject in the previous school, how the topic (and this great woman) was treated with such triviality, to the point where she was never even discussed in class.

As I have meditated on these experiences through the years, I have come to understand many of the underlying factors in racial tensions that still exist in America today. Again, this brought me to conclude that many times black people can be ***overly sensitive*** to racial issues due to their social conditioning and even educational experiences, and that white people are usually ***insensitive*** for the same reasons. Consequently, I have formed an opinion (expressed in two parts) as to a potential solution to the problem, which I want to share with you for your consideration:

First, that slavery, the oppression of blacks, and especially the atrocities committed against them should be treated in a distant-historical manner (instead of emotionally) when taught in predominately black schools. Instead, I suggest that an emphasis of their deliverance from that past (not a present continued legacy of that oppression), and the history of the Civil Rights Movement *in the light of positive advancements and its great leaders,* should be taught. Additionally, they should be taught a broader sense of American and world histories so that they can gain a perspective of the world that does not focus all their attention on themselves and their own racial background (which only fosters selfishness, segregation, and resentment.) We are not "islands unto ourselves" and need to see ourselves as a part of the overall population, appreciating our place within it, no matter what our cultural or racial heritage.

Furthermore, I believe also there needs to be taught to America's black youth an emphasis on the many white persons of American history who opposed slavery and its institution, thereby causing its downfall. History tells us that there were many who actively sought to end slavery in America for various reasons—some political, some economic, and many on moral grounds. There were an abundance of Christians who had white skin that opposed slavery and participated in its downfall, such as the Quakers and Abraham Lincoln, for example. These things need to be taught to America's black children and youth so that they understand that both historically and even now, white people were both part of the problem *and* the solution. A balanced perspective on this issue will help them as adults to determine how to identify and cooperate with those Caucasians who endeavor to end the bigotry and injustices continuing to linger in our society—and the many who are sympathetic to such a cause. Working together, we *can* make a difference!

Frederick Douglass worked alongside many white abolitionists in his day and developed friendships with many influential white people, including Abraham Lincoln himself. He understood that it was not white men ***categorically*** that was the problem, but the institution of slavery and ignorant bigotry in general. Therefore, he sought allies among white men and women of a similar mindset in his work as an abolitionist. Similarly, African American adults today need to "team up" with those of us of white skin color (disregarding political affiliation, I might add) to solve the remaining Civil Rights issues present in America. Teaching a righteous and balanced view of history to our children and youth will go a long way to ensure that they will be properly equipped for the challenges of the future in winning this fight for true equality and racial harmony in America and the world.

The second point to my opinion on these matters is that these same historical subjects, particularly the atrocities and oppression of the African Americans along with the history of the Civil Rights Movement, should be *emphasized* in the predominately white schools. They need to learn about Harriet Tubman, Frederick Douglass, and Dred Scott. White children and youth should be immersed into the historical facts of the slave trade, the Underground Railroad, and the Civil Rights Movement of the 1950's and 60's. Given a proper historical perspective of these important events of our history, today's white American youth would grow into adulthood with a greater sense of appreciation for African Americans and sensitivity to the issues that are important to them. Then they also can become part of America's solution to any remaining Civil Rights issues that may exist in the future.

My conclusion is that if these things I have expressed above were done, then African Americans would and could be *less* sensitive to racial issues, while white folks would become *more* sensitive to them. The result, I believe, would be a society that is more balanced, mutually respectful, and which works together to solve America's racial problems and injustices. I understand that you may not agree with me. However, the educational changes I suggested above are my personal opinion as to a possible "fix" for the problems discussed. It is an opinion based on years of observation, study of Scripture, and the story I am sharing with you in this book. In any case, it is a perspective worth considering within the context of the story that formed it, and I hope you will do so.

Without a doubt, however, we need to find a way to close this chasm of misunderstanding that exists between the different ethnic groups of this country. We need to build a bridge over the "Sensitivity Divide".

CHAPTER 7

Bridging the "Sensitivity Divide"

As I stated previously, black folks often tend to be over-sensitive while white folks tend to be insensitive. I call this distance between them the "Sensitivity Divide". This "divide" varies in size from situation to situation depending on the people involved and circumstances encountered. Everybody has his own "sensitivity level" in regards to both himself and those of other races and cultures. It is the difference between those levels of sensitivity that often determine whether one is offended or not, whether any real offense was intended or not.

Let me give you a scenario for an example that could apply to people from various racial backgrounds. An *overly* sensitive African American comes into contact with an ignorant and <u>insensi</u>tive white person. As they interact with one another, the black person takes offense as the white person violates racial taboos in his or her ignorance. The African American walks away thinking "redneck!" or "what a bigot!" while the Caucasian walks away *not even knowing anything is wrong*! It has been my experience both personally as a white person immersed into a black culture and setting, as well as observationally through the years, that much of what is *perceived* as "racist" by many black Americans is simply the *ignorance* of the white person of racial issues, not any real animosity directed toward them. This proved to be the case in my own situation, and I know it to be in many others.

Let me share a great example from my personal life to illustrate this further: When I was attending this same Mills E. Godwin High School, I happened to walk up behind a female friend of mine one Monday afternoon and put my hand on her shoulder to draw her attention so we could converse. She immediately reacted quite angrily against the contact, "Ouch! Don't touch me I have a sunburn!". Her reaction to me was as if the sunburn was my entire fault! The fact that my contact with her *resulted* in pain is not justification to blame me *for* the pain. **She** laid out in the sun too long that weekend and **she** hid the sunburn with clothing to such an extent that I had no indication it was there prior to touching her shoulder. My contact with her was nothing more than what would normally be considered a harmless "tap".

This illustrates my point...many times people touch us in areas of our lives and self-image that are overly sensitive due to past trauma, social conditioning, or some other influences. We all too often react to them in a most angry or offended manner because of the pain we feel, not really recognizing that the existence of the pain is evidence that something is wrong in *us*...not *them*. They may have "touched" us, but it was our own hidden issues that were the real *source* of the pain.

In racial situations, I have been on the "offending" end of such social contact when I was totally ignorant of the enhanced sensitivity that was present in the other person's mind and emotions. In the case of my school experiences early in life, this resulted in being branded a "racist" by the offended person while I was still scratching my head trying to figure out what I had said or done to tick him/her off.

Similarly, I have witnessed many such episodes between other people through the years and seen the pain and bitterness certain African Americans experienced toward white folks, when many times the white folks did not mean any harm at all. We have to bridge the Sensitivity Divide! We have to take responsibility for our own hearts, attitudes and actions so that we will both be less likely to *be* offended by others in their ignorance, and more apt to appreciate the races and cultures around us so that we do not cause offenses to others. We also need to make an effort to close the Sensitivity Divide for the next generation through changes in our educational priorities, as I mentioned before, so that their struggle will be an easier one than our own.

"Are you saying that there are no true white bigots? Are you saying there is no such thing as racism among white folks? Are you saying that it is all in our heads?"

No, not at all. Notice I said above "many times"—not "every time". I have been the witness of many truly racist acts or statements made by white people toward black folks. I will be discussing a couple of them in the next chapter, but for right now, let us stick with my current subject.

Let's just face it...white folks in America are, for the most part, clueless when it comes to races other than themselves. In fact, this is generally true about any race on the planet, unless they have been influenced or forced into learning the other race's culture.

I have actually been in situations where a black person (and in one case, a black minister) was ranting and raving about those "racist white folks" generically, or perhaps in a denomination, political party or other group. As I have listened to them, I found that the person who was proving to be a "racist" was actually the one doing the ranting and raving!

"How could that be?"

My Microsoft Encarta 98 Encyclopedia software on my computer defines racism as : **"Racism,** making the race of other people a factor in attitudes or actions concerning them." [1]

This person is categorically calling either all white folks, or all the white folks in a certain group as "racists" or "bigots" who are against the black man. Obviously, his or her "attitudes or actions concerning them" are based on the race of those people. Simply because of the color of their skin, he or she is concluding that they are racists. Therefore, by definition, the one who draws such an assumption is actually the racist. It is no different than if the white guy said, "All black people are criminals." Same issue, conduct, and attitude. Both are racist statements, and neither is true...just a matter of prejudice and ignorance of the race being discussed.

Let me make another point here: **racism by any other name is still racism**. Calling it "black rage" or some other label may make you *feel* better about it, but it is still racism if it makes "the race of other people a factor in attitudes or actions concerning them." I have actually heard it said by black persons that it is impossible for a black man or woman to be a racist since he or she is black. I'm not sure what dictionary they're using to define "racist", but it seems to me that someone who professes such a ridiculous notion has either lost touch with reality or simply will not admit the truth. ***Truth denied is not truth negated***. The color of one's skin is not the determining factor in defining a racist—it is his attitude and actions toward people of other races that exposes his racism, no matter what his complexion. Any other position on this subject is ignorance at best—and in reality nothing more than denial and self-deception to avoid taking responsibility for one's own bitterness and hate. No matter what your own racial background, any animosity you feel toward any other person because of his or her race, or color, is racism—and you need to deal with that issue in your own heart and life.

Some Additional History

While we are on the subject of "history" as we left off in my

Bridging the "Sensitivity Divide"

story, I thought this might be a good place to share a few historical facts that you can easily verify in your public library or the Internet. Since I have made such an issue about the lack of teaching in the areas of slavery, black oppression, and Civil Rights in predominately-white schools, it seems just and good to address some history that is seemingly omitted in most of the predominately-black schools also. Perhaps a little history lesson can help a few of my African American friends to find healing for some racial bitterness and resentment.

Of course, I will be covering some history later that will help my Caucasian readers further understand some of these sensitive issues, but right here I want to highlight again that not all white people in America were against the black folks or Civil Rights.

For example, there are the Quakers. These were religious Christian white folks who originally started the Underground Railroad in the 1780's because they were morally outraged by slavery of any person. They were particularly sympathetic to the plight of the Negro slaves and began this whole system of escape to transport them to free states. It was quickly dominated for the most part by free Negroes within a short time, however, and grew rapidly due to the hard work and labor of black leaders such as Harriet Tubman.

There was William Lloyd Garrison, who in 1831 founded *The Liberator*, an abolitionist newspaper in Boston, Massachusetts. Historians cite that event as the true beginning of the Abolitionist Movement here in America, for his publication, as well as the American Anti-slavery Society he helped form in 1833, fostered the organized growth of abolitionism.

We already mentioned Harriet Beecher Stowe, the white Christian woman abolitionist. For that matter, most of the Abolitionists of the North were white folks, and most of them were Christians. They varied in their motives for ending slavery from political grounds to serious moral objections, but it was all for the ultimate benefit of the Negroes.

Again, there was Abraham Lincoln, the white Christian President who was mightily used by God to abolish slavery with the help of the white Republican controlled congress.

In the Twentieth Century, just to be more recent, during the term of President Dwight D. Eisenhower, a white Christian (who also happened to be Republican), school desegregation was ordered by the Supreme Court in the case of Brown vs. Board of Education. Desegregation was then enforced by President Eisenhower in Arkansas with Federal troops and he signed the Civil Rights Act of 1957 into law.

So you see, there were quite a few white folks who were trying to help the black folks out for a variety of reasons, particularly the Christian white folks...and for that matter, the Republicans also.

CHAPTER 8

Political Racism

There is a prolific form of "reverse racism" in the African American population that needs to be addressed in some detail if we are to have a fairly complete discussion of bigotry as it exists in America today. This variety of prejudice, though often ignored, exists within the black community because of their historic tendency to blend religion, politics, and ethnicity within their culture. Because of the ethnic topics we tackle within the context of my personal biography, this book would not be complete without confronting this issue also.

The discrimination I am discussing here is the tendency for many in the black community to equate their cultural and racial identity as an *African American* with their support of the *Democratic Party*. By so doing, they often view Republicans as "white racists" and enemies to Civil Rights, while also labeling black Republicans as traitors, or "Uncle Tom's". This is a source of great misunderstanding and conflict, and serves only to undermine any further advancements of the Civil Rights cause.

Let it be understood, however, that in addressing this issue, my motives are love and reconciliation. If we are to see true harmony within our country, then all the walls of resentment and hostility need to be broken down. To accomplish this, I will need to take some time "punching holes" through those walls, and in so doing, may appear to be endorsing one party over the other. However, this is not to be construed as an "endorsement" of any political party, but rather an attempt to reconcile differences by setting the record straight. Therefore, I ask you please to read my comments here with an open mind and receptive heart to hear the love intended, especially if you happen to be African American by racial origin.

Shocking News

I was invited to sit in on a minister's meeting one day as a guest observer. The meeting was convened by the leader of this predominately black ministerial organization for the purpose of discussing with the leadership his intentions to publicly endorse the Republican Party. He was sharing his heart with these men and women to prepare them for any questions directed to them from black Christians concerning his public stand. "Once people begin hear what I am saying out there," he told them, "they may want to know from you why I am doing this. Therefore, I don't want you to be caught off guard."

As he was making his statements concerning why he supported the Republican platform and was revealing himself openly as a black Republican, one of the other ministers kept interjecting at various points, "But, all Republicans are white bigots!" Repeatedly, this brother showed his bewilderment at his leader's political affiliation and intent by repeating this statement at various intervals of the discussion. As I sat and listened to this brother's astonished objections, I could not help but think, "This brother needs some understanding so that he can find some peace with his brethren." My personal experiences gave me a perspective this brother really needed to hear.

It was in that meeting that I first shared publicly my testimony of race and culture as you have been reading through until this point. I wanted this brother, and the other men and women present, to realize that much of what they perceived as bigotry in white people was actually only ignorance. The positive response I received from those wonderful ministers following the meeting were actually the catalyst that resulted in me writing the book *White Man In A Black Man's World*.

Who's The Bigot?

Actually, the real bigotry was primarily found in that *racist* statement, "All Republicans are white bigots!" While it may be true at the present that most Republicans are white (but for that matter, most Democrats are white too—Caucasians happen to be the majority in this country), many Republicans, including the leader of that group, are black. Additionally, many are Hispanic, Oriental, and various other minority ethnic groups. To assume that they are all "white", and especially that most are "bigots", is essentially a racist stereotype that is not supported by either history, or modern reality.

We should hate racism in any form–and this version of discrimination is just as wrong **and *ignorant*** as any other form. It is not any more righteous for a black man or woman to spew out racially prejudiced propaganda against any people or group than it would be for the reverse to happen...is it? I think not. Politically motivated racism in the black community against Republicans (those white and black) is a divisive stumbling block America could really do without—that is if we want to see progress.

This form of bigotry seems all-too-often encouraged by many in the Democratic Party itself to guarantee their voting base and discredit their Republican opponents—when they should be dealing with social issues in a *constructive* manner. My friend, *the object is not winning the election,* ***but to promote the welfare of the people!*** I truly wish more politicians from both parties would figure that out!

As I had mentioned previously in this book, the Republican Party was the political catalyst that ended slavery. It was also the Republican president, Abraham Lincoln, who penned the Emancipation Proclamation and pushed through the 13th Amendment to the Constitution, forever ending slavery. Though often slandered by some today because of his evolving political and social views of blacks during his presidential career, Abraham Lincoln was morally opposed to slavery and Civil Rights abuses from the beginning. History records that his earlier positions regarding emancipation and the plight of the black slaves was "toned down" for both political reasons and what he perceived to be the social realities of his day. The fact is that Lincoln needed to "sell" abolition to the white population to be elected, and furthermore to conduct the war that subsequently erupted. He even publicly advocated deportation of the slaves back to Africa early in his candidacy and first presidential term as a solution to the question of what to do with them once slavery was abolished. The racial prejudice so prevalent around him caused him to conclude that full citizenship and integration for the black population could not work in America. However, Lincoln's later views had evolved through his relationships with black abolitionists, and the courage of black Union soldiers, to one that advocated total citizenship and even voting rights for the African American population. It was, in fact, his views along these lines expressed in a speech from a White House balcony on April 11, 1865 in the hearing of southern supporter and racist John Wilkes Booth that lead to his assassination three days later.

Furthermore, following the Civil War and the death of Lincoln,

Political Racism

the Republicans controlled the Congress of the United States and, through Reconstruction, the governments of the South. Most of them were avid abolitionists who shared Lincoln's later views of citizenship, social equality, and voting rights for the newly liberated black population. During this time, they passed the first Civil Rights Act in 1866 and subsequently the 14th Amendment, which made the provisions of the Civil Rights Act a part of the Constitution and guaranteed citizenship rights for blacks. They also passed the 15th Amendment in 1869 (which was ratified in 1870), which broadened the 14th Amendment's protection of Civil Rights for blacks by assuring them the right to vote, and passed yet another Civil Rights Act in 1875. Republicans even elected many blacks to public office, particularly in the South, much to the dismay of the former Confederates.

Following the end of Reconstruction in 1877, the Democrats (who were running a pro-slavery campaign prior to the war) regained control of the South and began reversing many of the initiatives previously done by the Republicans. Although they could not change the Constitution itself, they began to reverse the application of many of these constitutionally protected rights for blacks in the South through segregation laws.

"What?"

That's right, the party that most African Americans think is the bastion of Civil Rights protection was the cause of much of the discrimination that necessitated the Civil Rights Movement of the 1950's and 1960's.

Groups such as the Ku Klux Klan (which was formed at the close of the Civil war by former Confederate generals) and mobs of southern white bigots used violence and intimidation to get blacks out of political offices and away from voting booths. Thousands of blacks were killed along with numerous pro-Negro whites. These violent hordes were themselves virtually all

Democrats by party affiliation.

Segregation laws and other anti-black laws were increasingly passed in the South and eventually the whole country, pushed forward by the Democratic Party. Did you know that most white racists, particularly the Ku Klux Klan, have historically voted Democrat? In fact, Microsoft's Encarta Encyclopedia says, "The Klan and other white terrorist groups directed their violence against black landowners, politicians, and community leaders, as well as whites who supported the Republican Party or racial equality." [1]

The historical truth is: among African Americans who voted, virtually **all** voted <u>Republican</u>, the party of Lincoln, until the 1930's when Roosevelt came along offering "a new deal". In fact, the Republican Party was ***the*** party of the American black man until Roosevelt. It could be said then that the Civil Rights efforts of the Democratic Party in the last 40 or so years simply reversed the trend they had **caused** in the previous 80 or more years.

As I stated before, I am not trying to bash the Democratic Party by writing all this. We needed to expose these elements of history to obtain a more accurate view of these political parties, for the purpose of racial reconciliation in regards to political affiliation. Many African Americans are unfamiliar with the wonderful Civil Rights history of the Republican Party. Therefore, they are susceptible to harboring unfounded resentment toward people they should not.

I am thankful that the Democratic Party did begin to "rise to the occasion" in the 1950's and 1960's as they adopted the Civil Rights cause and enacted many changes now reflected in America. Many good righteous men and women have stood up among the Democrats for the Civil Rights of minorities in America. An example is the Democratic president, Lyndon Johnson, who signed the Civil Rights Act of 1964.

Again, I do not intend to glorify the Republican Party with this book. I am sure, as with any organization of its size, that there are a few real "bona fide bigots" floating around in there (although I firmly believe that most who have been labeled such by Democrats emphatically are not). But, the same could probably be said of the Democratic Party as well, considering its historical record.

Let us forget the political rhetoric and move forward with progress in the issues that challenge our country today. That means we all need to work together to see positive change occur, no matter what our color...or political party affiliation. Therefore, let the African American community abandon its stereotyping of Republican politicians and candidates, because the historical record just does not support it.

Additionally, current events do not support such a racist branding of the Republican Party any more than history does. New black leaders have risen within the Republican Party and are now filling key cabinet positions in the administration of recently elected President George W. Bush. These African Americans (such as Secretary of State Colin Powell and National Security Adviser Condoleezza Rice) are some of the greatest examples of the new leaders that are moving to the forefront of black leadership in America. They are role models to be emulated by aspiring African American youth and adults alike and they should not scorned by other so-called "black leaders" who are threatened by their strong political views.

Additionally, as the story I related before indicates, many black clergy are endorsing Republican candidates and many are publicly advocating a move within the African American community to reconsider their political and economic choices. These black ministers have taken bold public stands to promote a "two-party" system in the black community, realizing that putting "all the eggs in one basket" is dangerous for the future of African American prosperity and Civil Rights. Therefore, let me say again that not all the

Republicans are even white; much less can anyone accurately say that they are all bigots.

My friend, it is time for you to stop buying the fear and character assassinations of good men and women that are being peddled by those who want to control your vote. It is time to take a good look at the facts and issues with a clear, open mind and make decisions for yourself. If they are good candidates for office, they should not have to "scare" you into voting for them for fear that the "white Republican bigots" are going take your job and Civil Rights. The daughter of one black minister reportedly began to cry uncontrollably when it was announced that George W. Bush had been elected president. When her father asked her what is wrong, she said, "They're going to make us all slaves again!" It is ridiculous that such ideas are spread throughout the black community, and even more tragic that people actually think it is true.

Let me note again, however, that I do not care if you are a Democrat or Republican...that is your choice. I *do* care if you are participating in reverse or politically-motivated racism and its resulting slander simply because of a person's political affiliation. Calling a black person, an "Uncle Tom" or a white person a "bigot" simply because he is a Republican is wrong. Period.

Furthermore, I *do* care if you are just simply following the "herd" like a blind man, without really ever investigating the issues and true facts surrounding them. If you find that your personal convictions and beliefs are best supported by a Democratic candidate because you have studied the issues and verified the facts concerning the candidates, then vote for him or her. However, if they are better supported by the Republican, you should be informed enough and bold enough to "buck the trend" and vote your conscience instead of listening to the racist "black propaganda" often put forth by some members of the Democratic Party and its supporters.

Politics is really not the issue here, **righteousness is**, and this type of behavior is slander at best, and blatant racism at worst. Remember the definition of racism? **"Racism**, making the race of other people a factor in attitudes or actions concerning them."[2] I do not think it is far off to say that making the party affiliation of other people a basis for judging their feelings toward race and Civil Rights issues is also a form of racism.

Nor is it too far off to say it is a form of racism if a person is labeled a "racist" simply because he or she disagrees with the convictions, agenda, or public record of a person who happens to be African American or Hispanic. One is not a bigot simply because he opposes specific minority men and women *on the grounds of certain issues*. Everybody has a right to disagree and not be labeled a "racist" for doing so. Only when they oppose minority men and women categorically could one say that their record may indicate bigotry.

My friend, if you are a Democrat, *be a moral one* and refuse to participate in character assassination of good people. Solicit votes based on real discussions of real issues instead of peddling fear and racial prejudices.

And for that matter, if you are a Republican, make sure that issues concerning Civil Rights are high on your list of priorities. Republicans should be doing more and more to bring about racial harmony within their own party as well as in this country. Their reputation for the last thirty or so years has not been exemplary in this subject area, so great strides need to be made within the party to change this. It is time for the Republican *reputation* to come up to the level of their wonderful *history* when it comes to being proactive in racial and cultural issues. Civil Rights and economic empowerment of minorities need to be high on their agenda.

The new "Compassionate Conservatism" of the President George W. Bush administration is definitely on the right track, and the progress I have seen is fast moving in the right direction. Given time, I believe the entire party (including the "old timers") will assimilate much of this new way of thinking into their own behavior as they become more racially and culturally aware. The new influx of prestigious African American and Hispanic leaders into the party will further accelerate this change in party attitude and reputation.

It is good to see the Republican Party coming up to speed on racial issues. This is beneficial for America and its entire population, because we truly do need to become a "two-party system" in regards to racial and cultural issues such as Civil Rights. For then and only then are we **truly** on our way to fulfilling Dr. King's dream of a country where its people are judged by the content of their character and not the color of their skin.

CHAPTER 9

Teaching Mike?

Having taken the side journeys of the previous two chapters to explore race, history and politics, it's time to return to my story and find out some additional lessons I was able to learn in life.

God's providence not only brought me to Mills E. Godwin High School, but it also caused me to have certain relationships there that would affect me greatly. My group of friends included other teens that were Jewish and black as well as us "mutts". Some of these friends taught me through our relationship some important issues about race, culture and of course racism.

One of those friends was Mike. Mike was racially a black guy, but as I said before about most of the black folks at this school, he was not culturally "black" like those of John Marshall. In Mike's case, he was raised all his life around the Caucasian culture. He went to school with white folks, virtually all his friends were either white or culturally white African Americans, and he even dated white girls almost exclusively. You see, Mike was a "black white-guy". His sister could be similarly culturally identified, except she was a freshman and we were seniors. Racially black but culturally white, my friend Mike was and is a good example of how "race"

White Man...in a Black Man's World

alone is only skin-deep.

Contrastingly, I have met folks, usually teens, who were white according to their skin color, but black according to their culture. Usually, when I have met such a teen and said something like, "Hello," they look at me like "what planet did you come from?" They cannot relate to me at all simply because of my skin color...they need some **cultural connection** with which they can identify in order to trust me and for us to communicate effectively.

When I have reverted to some of my former "ethnicity" training and said, "Yo, man! Wassup?" with a hip-hop type strut in my walk, they have begun to communicate with me in return. Why? They could relate to that. Again, though they were white by skin color, they were actually black by **culture**, and my pale skin was not sufficient to build a communication bridge. Likewise, Mike would occasionally have a real problem in communicating and relating to African Americans who were culturally "black".

One day I was talking with Mike outside his apartment building in the parking lot and he was telling me that he and his family were going to a family reunion that they had every couple of years or so.

"I hate going to these things," he said.

"Why?" I asked.

"Because I can't understand a thing any of my cousins say!" He was not kidding either—he was being quite serious.

I could not help but laugh about it though, "Oh, I'll teach you whatever you need to know Mike! You will do just fine." We both laughed.

His parents were what I call *culturally versatile*. They could hang with anybody of either cultural background without any problem. His dad could put on some really cool "brother talk" when he wanted to. I presume his siblings and other relatives were quite culturally African American, and he probably came from that heritage but ended up working with and living around white folks to

Teaching Mike?

such a degree that it was about all his kids knew. It probably was a result of his years in Germany with the Army. This may be supposition on my part, but the results were clear as to how Mike and his sister turned out.

Actually, Mike used to kid around that I knew more about "being black" than he did! For example, Mike and I would often go on "cruises" through the shopping mall looking for "chicks". I do not know why we did that so often, we never actually had a conversation with any of the girls we saw there... we just walked around trying to look 'cool'! I guess we were waiting for them to blow us kisses or something. Funny... they never did. I find it entertaining also that when I go to the mall now, I can see groups of teens doing the same thing today.

Anyway, on one such "cruise" we happened to walk by a store that had a boom box outside its doorway playing some rap music. I hardly noticed and kept walking by, but Mike stopped and called up to me, "Hey Richard!"

I stopped and looked back, "What?"

Pointing at the boom box he asked, "Do I like this music?"

I answered, "Yeah, Mike! You're black, you love that kind of music."

With that comment, he jokingly started to walk away from it with an obviously African American "strut" as if trying to be culturally "black" for a moment. We both laughed our way down the mall corridor continuing our vain "cruise" for girls. At least we entertained ourselves while we wasted our time there.

I have found that race, and particularly the color of your skin, has little to nothing to do with your mindset or view of the world, but rather it is your *cultural heritage* that determines much of your way of thinking. You can be Asian American, for example, and be culturally "white American" in most ways unless you just came over to this country or your family lives within an Asian community.

Likewise, you can be black or white according to your skin color and be the opposite according to your culture. It just depends on where you grow up and around whom.

I have also found that culture can be *learned* and absorbed through association. Many black folks, for example, have easily learned and perhaps adopted a "white American" cultural mindset or habits due to their choice of career or perhaps the environment in which they grew up...like Mike.

Caucasian people also, in my opinion, would do well to hang out with a few black folks and pick up some of their cultural habits. It's like food in some ways. Just like adding some seasoning to your food makes things taste better, learning how to be a little "black" can make life much more interesting!

I truly enjoy having a "beat" to my gospel music, and putting hot sauce on my fried chicken! I can dance too, when the choir gets me goin'! Glory to God! My black brothers and sisters at church have even called me a "white black-guy" before. One sister actually said, "Aw, Reverend Vermillion, you're not really white!" To which I replied "Actually, I'm a black man trapped in a white man's body!" Everybody in the room just lost it laughing.

I really do like what that one white preacher had said, "I'm not as white as I used to be, but I'm not as black as I want to be!" Amen, brother!

Cultural Adaptation

Black folks historically in this country have learned the "do's and don'ts" of how to deal with white people, primarily out of necessity years ago. There was a time in this country that it could be quite dangerous to their health, and perhaps family, if a black person stepped on some white toes, so to speak. Many a good black man and woman have been "lynched" because of some white folks who did not like how they were acting.

Teaching Mike?

In the November, 2000 issue of *Charisma & Christian Life* magazine, there was a very bold and shocking article entitled "The History America Chose to Forget" by Valerie G. Lowe. The article chronicled the story of black lynchings in American history and the stories of several of those who were lynched, including pictures taken of the lynchings, drawing attention to a New York gallery exhibit curated by James Allen, who had collected the photos and stories for over fifteen years.[1]

The *Charisma* article told of a man named July Perry, who was lynched in 1920 in the state of Florida for having the "audacity" to exercise his constitutional right to vote.

There was also Rubin Stacey, who was hanged in 1935 for scaring a white woman when he asked her for food.

Another victim was William Brown, who was accused (not convicted or even tried in court) for molesting a white girl and was hanged, shot, mutilated and burned in 1919 in Omaha, Nebraska.

In fact, 3,436 people were reported lynched in America between 1889 and 1922 according to the article, and another source they cited says that there were 4,730 lynched between 1882 and 1968. Mind you, these were just the reported cases....there were undoubtedly much more than that not reported.

The thing that impacted me the most about this article was the pictures of crowds of white people—smiling and acting as if they were attending a carnival—standing around the mutilated bodies that were hanging by ropes! The brutality chronicled by the article also included that the victims were often tortured, and that many times fingers were cut off one by one and distributed to bystanders as souvenirs.

I kept asking myself as I read the article and looked at the gruesome pictures, "Where were the ministers? Where were the preachers? Where was the conviction of sin?" I am shaken to the core of my being that the "white" ministers of that time were not emphatically preaching against such atrocities. Jesus' attitude about the human race has not changed since He walked the shores of Galilee and died on the Cross for the salvation of all humanity. The fact that it could be such a public spectacle and circus is evidence of the depravity of the clergy at that time. Murderous mobs killing innocent people without opposition from the clergy or conviction of sin. In my mind, this puts the greatest burden of guilt on those who should have known better and made an effort to stop the brutality—the pastors and other members of the clergy. It pains me to think it, but I cannot help but guess that not a few of them were even involved.

Unrepented sin **will** be accounted for...eventually. It does not matter who perpetrated it, or who condoned it by their actions, words or for that matter, their apathy. The Bible clearly says that God's books shall be opened, and every man will give account of himself for what he has done here on the Earth...even professing Christians and so-called ministers.

"Yeah, but that was a long time ago!" someone might protest. "They don't do such things in America today!"

Well, how about Raynard Johnson, the 17-year-old boy who was found hanged from a tree in Mississippi on June 16, 1999? The police ruled it "suicide" that this bright young honor student was found in such a condition. However, when I visited Mississippi the following October, my uncle, who lives down there (and is white) said that it was the general opinion of the community that he was lynched because he was dating a white girl.

No, the monstrous hate that was public policy and practice in the late nineteenth and early twentieth century (as well as before) does still exist in pockets here and there in this country. The only difference is that though some people may **want** to do some of these things still to African Americans, fortunately the laws and general public opinion make it very dangerous for them to do it—most of the time.

White folks in this country do need to wake up to the realities of racism in America and become more culturally aware of the pain and history of the African American men and women. If they did, then they would not say some of the stupid things they do or act the way they sometimes can. In fact, a few of them might even "wise up" and start going to a "predominately-black" church and learn how to have some fun in their worship for a change! (Dear God, you have *got* to be tired of singing *Bringing in the Sheaves*! Most of you do not even know what a "sheave" is!)

I commend *Charisma & Christian Life* magazine for the boldness to publish such an exposing article, and I hope many "white" Americans, especially Christians, were impacted by it. Perhaps as a result of reading this book, many will pick up copies of the article reprint from the publisher, or view it online, and grow from the knowledge and experience. I truly hope so.

It can readily be seen why black folks in this country, especially the South, have had a history of being sensitive and mindful to not cross certain racial boundaries and offend white people's cultural views in order to avoid retribution. Even today, it seems to be a cultural thing in the African American community to adapt easily to a "white" environment. It is quite common to find only one black person in a setting with mostly white people—on the job, for example.

It is also quite common to find a small handful of black folks in a predominately-white church. I have visited many "white" churches and have seen only an extremely small percentage of black folks there. For that matter, I have also been to churches that were anywhere from 20% to 70% "black" and actually had a "white" pastor leading them.

What I want to see considerably more of is "predominately-black" churches with "black" pastors, which have a significant number of "white" Christians being bold enough to worship there.

It is a whole lot less common to see it that way, but I think things are changing. A "predominately-white" congregation with a "black" pastor would be even more awesome to see!

By God's providence, I actually met a distant cousin of mine on the Internet who, by appearances, is also a "white man in a black man's world."

My cousin, Rod Vermillion, and I bumped into each other online when he came across an advertisement of mine and saw my last name. He dropped me an e-mail to say "hi" and we fast became close buddies as we found out the amazing similarities we had with each other!

In addition to both of us being handsome guys with beards who are married to beautiful wives (not that I am biased, mind you), it turns out that Rod himself is also a minister! He once was the head of security at Bishop Carlton Pearson's church, Higher Dimensions, a predominately-black church there in Tulsa, Oklahoma! (Apparently, it just runs in the family to hang out with "black folks" in church.) He has since moved on in ministry to become the Associate Pastor of a wonderful church in Ohio, where he hopes to help them integrate their congregation more than they have experienced in the past.

Rod got a later start in life than I did as a "white man in a black man's world". He was an adult when the Lord started exposing him to these things, so he still has to work on his rhythm as he learns to clap on the right beat, but at least he has learned how to dress right being around the black folks! Praise the Lord! You see, miracles **can** happen! Just kidding...well, maybe.

Back to Mike......

He and I did learn a few things about racial and cultural issues together. In fact, we shared a couple of outright face-to-face confrontations with racism. These were situations, unfortunately, where my good friend was discriminated against simply because of the color of his skin. Regrettably, the first incident involved my own grandfather.

Pop's Fudge

I dearly loved my eccentric grandfather. He and his wife (my step-grandmother) basically raised me the first year of my life as my parents struggled to transition from a military life to the civilian work force. They lived with him my first year and he and his wife took care of me most of every day. Because of this, we were always close.

We did not really talk much at all about black folks or race issues. Since the family was all white folks, it did not really seem to come up much. He did make a few comments about "Negroes" and "black people" from time to time, but I didn't really pick up on the disdain he had for them socially since he never used the "n———r" word that I can recall.

He had many different black people who worked for him before I came on the scene since he had owned a business. Some worked for his company while others at the house as maids and such. He mentioned occasionally taking a few of the men with him hunting for deer down in the Williamsburg area where some of my family owned property, so I never deduced any malice toward people of color since he seemed to be comfortable around them. Apparently, as long as they were in a servant-type position, they were okay, but you did not "socialize with them". However, I had not picked up on this portion of his opinion about African Americans until after I had violated his cultural conditioning.

Mike was just simply my friend. He was just "Mike". Like Tony, I did not really consciously think of him as "black", just…"Mike". A friend is a friend, no matter what the color of his skin. The fact that Mike was culturally a "white guy" made it even more difficult to think of the color of his skin and racial background. He was just simply..."Mike."

One day, I got the bright idea while we were driving around, "Hey, let's go over to my grandfather's house and I'll introduce you to him. He makes the best fudge in the world and we can get some while we are there!" Sounded great to Mike, so off to Pop's house we went (that is what we called him).

I brought him in, introduced him to my grandfather, and told Mike again about Pop's fudge in front of my grandfather saying, "Hey Pop! Could you give us some fudge so that Mike can taste how good it is? I told him all about it!" I figured he would be honored that I thought so highly of his fudge that I actually brought somebody over to try some.

"I don't have any for you," he replied.

I thought it was quite strange that he did not have any. He **always** had fudge!

Then I noticed, he was not talking very much to me or Mike—that was also very unusual. He just had this very tense grin pasted on his face as he quietly stared at us. I started to get quite uncomfortable, and so was Mike. I began to realize the atmosphere in the room was extremely tense and that there was something wrong with my grandfather. His attitude was strange and he was acting very weird. I decided to make a quick exit.

"Oh, well. I am sorry you're out of fudge Pop. Maybe next time," I said as I began my exit with Mike.

He did not say much. Just had this tense grin. "Goodbye" he said.

When we got outside, I apologized to Mike, "Hey man, I don't know what just happened in there, but I'm sorry. I do not understand it, he **always** has fudge. The whole thing was kind of weird, including how my grandfather was acting."

"That's okay," he said. But I knew that he had been hurt by the whole incident. The tension of the visit seemed to be directed

Teaching Mike?

toward Mike for some strange reason, but I did not have a clue at the time what it was.

That night when I got home, my father asked me "Did you take Mike over to visit Pop?"

"Yes," I answered "It was so strange...," still not fully understanding what had happened.

He replied, "Don't ever take Mike over there again! He called me right after you left and chewed me out on the phone for an hour on 'how dare I let my son hang out with black friends'!"

I was shocked! "That's what that was all about?" I exclaimed. I could not believe it! It just never occurred to me that in the end of the Twentieth Century someone could still be a segregationist like that!

Dad never had any issues with black folks himself, so I did not think of his father having any either. It just had never come up until then. However, I discovered through this incident that my grandfather did have some racist issues in his heart. He was a bigot. That really bothered me about him. I still loved him, but it hurt me that his thinking was so twisted in this area, and that he had discriminated against my good friend, simply because his skin was black.

I found out later that he did in fact have fudge there at the house when we visited, but "not for you." That hurt even more. I could also tell the whole situation hurt Mike somewhat too.

I do not know if Mike had ever really dealt directly with racism like that before that time. If he had, I did not know about it. Having grown up around white folks all his life, it seemed like Mike did not really even notice his own skin color either most of the time. Confronting an obviously hostile racist attitude was certainly not a fun experience for him. I could relate—having been through similar situations before in a reverse manner. I could understand how he felt, and I think that hurt me the most. Unfortunately, this was not the only, or the worst case we shared together.

A Little Off The Top, And Don't Touch The Color

After high school, I attended Virginia Commonwealth University for a couple years and decided to join the United States Marine Corps Reserve due in part to the influence of a couple of my fraternity brothers (I was still not a Christian). I returned to VCU and to living at home with my parents after I had completed my active duty training.

Mike had not really done anything the first couple of years after high school. He did attend the local community college off and on some. Suddenly, he up and decided to join the Marine Corps as active duty... sort of "out of the blue". He was gone over seas to Okinowa, Japan, for a while and was discharged after about a year or two in the Corps due to some medical issue.

At some point after he returned to the States, he and I decided to go and get a couple of haircuts together. I had been going to this barber down in Richmond city because he had been recommended to me by one of my Marine Corps buddies. He was a former Marine himself from the World War II era. He had fought in Iwa Gima and a couple of other of the South Pacific campaigns. In fact, that was how he got started as a barber–cutting other Marines' hair in the foxholes between battles to help keep everybody close to regulation.

He was a great barber to visit and talk with. Loving World War II history and being a Marine myself, I had a great respect for the man. I also enjoy spending time with the older generations because you can learn so much from their experiences, and I find their many stories quite interesting. Unfortunately, they can also have a few "hang ups" that might be unsavory.

I told Mike, "Let's go over to this barber shop. He is a former Marine vet and he gives great regulation haircuts. He has one special one he calls a 'tight around the rim' that I usually get." Sounded good to Mike, so off we went.

Teaching Mike?

I had not ever really noticed that, though the area where the barbershop was located was predominately black in population, only white folks had been coming into his shop. Most of them were elderly, like him, and I guess if I noticed at all, I must have thought that his clientele was mostly folks that liked listening to the 40's music on his radio in the shop.

When Mike and I walked in, there was one older white man sitting in one of the waiting chairs reading a newspaper and Mr. R. was doing some cleaning up around one of the barber chairs. He looked toward the door as he heard us walking in.

"Hey Mr. R.! My friend and I are here to get one of your famous 'tight around the rim' hair cuts" I said.

He looked shocked.

"I can't do that." he said, greatly confusing me in the process.

"What? Don't tell me your closing. I thought we had a couple more hours to spare." I replied.

"What I mean is I can't give *him* any service," pointing at Mike. "If I do that, then all *those people* in the area will expect me to do their hair."

I was aghast! Shocked! Bewildered! Even confused! I could not believe he had actually called Mike one of "those people". I could not believe he was **actually** refusing Mike service because of his race!

"But he's a Marine!" I protested.

"I don't care if he is." he replied. "I still can't give him a hair cut."

I looked over at the other "gentleman" seated against the wall in amazement as if to say, "Did you hear what I just heard?" He had this indignant look on his face like, "Who does he think he is bringing a n——r in here!" as he stared back at me in agreement with Mr. R's bigotry.

I was shocked. Mike was shocked. Both of us were shocked!

Without even a hasty "goodbye," we just left. If he couldn't do Mike's haircut, he can't do mine either!

Again, I really was hurting for Mike. "Hey man, I'm sorry for that. I had no idea..."

"Let's just leave," he replied. I could see the hurt and anger on his face. Who could blame him? We jumped in the car and took off.

I never really discussed that incident after that with Mike that I can remember...it was too painful for either of us to bring up again. However, I did learn a lesson in cultural racism from the experience. Two old men from a different era, still hanging on to racial bigotry that was prevalent during that time–but should be discarded today. Mike and I actually experienced a "time warp" back into the days of national segregation. We actually witnessed something that we had only heard of from bygone days—separate drinking fountains... "Go to the back of the bus"... "We don't do n——r's hair in here."

I could not have even imagined the suffering and humiliation that African Americans must have suffered during those times unless I had witnessed this piece of "segregation" still lingering in America toward the end of the twentieth century. The sad thing is that the man was in bondage to a mental mindset that separated himself from many wonderful people in the community in which he lived and worked in. His life could have been much richer if he (and those who frequented his business) could be liberated enough to see that the color of their skin is no reason to segregate yourself from another people or race. He could learn so much from the people he so disdained.

Not only that, but Mr. R was risking his entire business and personal assets by holding on to his outdated bigotry. If Mike had been so inclined, he could have "sued the man's pants off" and cost him the very business in which he refused to serve Mike! Civil Rights legislation that has been in law for over a hundred years

Teaching Mike?

would have guaranteed his win in court. Imagine the irony... refusing business to a black person and losing the business because of it. Some people need to learn things the "hard way" though, so a few will probably have to travel that road to find out that bigotry does not pay in the long run.

Mike, on the other hand, is not retributive in his personality and he preferred to just walk away and forget that man's ignorance and racism. Perhaps, like myself, he realized that the man was simply an ignorant "white" man from another era, and you often times "can't teach an old dog new tricks" if he has been set in his ways for sixty years or more. Sometimes, you are just simply better off walking away, for the offense and pain will grow much worse if you feed the bitterness with malice and retribution. Then, even if you "win" your fight, you lose yourself in the battle, and that kind of "victory" is not worth having.

Mike used to joke around that I taught him how to be a "black" guy. Perhaps, we were just both learning lessons in race, racism, and cultural differences together.

CHAPTER 10

Dark Red or Light?

I believe that one of the issues that often prevent different races and ethnic groups from getting along with each other is simply one of *perspective*. Like the old saying goes, "beauty is in the eye of the beholder." If we can change how we *view* ourselves and other races, we can change how we respond to them in the process. One of the greatest examples I can share with you is a lesson taught me by our government's most respected branch of the armed services (at least in my opinion), the United States Marine Corps.

Marine Learns Green

The racial tensions of the 1950's and especially the 60's had created the need for the Corps to devise a way of *decolorizing* the Marine population. With the end of segregated ranks, "color" and race became a real problem and needed a solution. Can you imagine a platoon that had mixed into it a couple of white redneck bigots and a few black folks with racial "chips on their shoulders"? It would be chaos!

They devised a method of "reprogramming" the mindset of the new recruits to eliminate racial prejudices, at least within the confines of their military duty, and implemented this training into the rigorous disciplining every new recruit underwent. It was a very simple, yet amazingly profound method that was devised, and one we can all learn from.

I began my Basic Training with a group of other young men back in May of 1988. Almost immediately upon our arrival at Paris Island, South Carolina, the drill instructors started grilling us with "there is only one color in the United States Marine Corps... **GREEN**! You are now **all** green! You are either light green or dark green... but **ALL** of you are now **green**!" This simple lesson on the color "green" was the Marine Corps' strategy to deal with racial issues and problems in its ranks. Despite its simplicity, this method was quite effective, and as we discussed before, quite necessary. Therefore, by focusing our attention on a single color of the spectrum—green, they basically eliminated "color" from the mind of the new recruits as soon as they arrived. Green was now the only color we were to recognize. If someone asked us what a person looked like, we answered, "He was a dark-green Marine" or "She was a light-green Marine." If they were in uniform, or if we knew them to be a Marine, they were just one shade of green or another in our eyes.

I know you may wonder if such a simple method could really work to quiet racial tensions within military ranks, but it really worked quite well! In fact, there were several white guys whom I perceived to be real "rednecks" in my platoon whose attitudes straightened up real quick once the "fun stuff" really began there at Paris Island. (By "fun stuff", I'm referring to mean-looking drill instructors screaming in your face at the top of their lungs, spraying you with spittle in the process—and a few other interesting things to go along with all that.) A couple of the black guys also experienced an attitude adjustment during that time, and all of them just saw "green" pretty quickly. Even after basic training, I saw on several occasions that once one of these ex-bigots realized that the other person was a Marine, all they saw was green and you would have thought they were "bosom buddies" even if they were of a different skin color. They may have still had some racial prejudice in their hearts—and in civilian settings even displayed it—but once they found out that the other person was a Marine, then all they could see was **green**.

Light green, dark green... they were all Marines... and that is all that really mattered to us. I guess that is part of why I was so shocked by the barbershop incident I had with Mike. "But he is a Marine" I had protested. However, Mr. R. was from a generation **prior** to the revelation of a one-color Marine Corps. In his day, this nation had a segregated military.

Lesson for the Church

For my Christian readers let me share that later in life, after I was born-again, the Lord reminded me of all this "green" stuff in my prayer time one day and spoke to my heart, "In My Church, there is only one color... **RED**... blood-red because all of My people are washed in My Blood. Therefore, a Christian is either a *light-red* Christian or a *dark-red* Christian, but they are all blood-red in My eyes." Wow! What a revelation for the Church of Jesus Christ to get a hold of! What a difference that could make!

I shared that with my wife and we often speak of Christians even today in those terms to one another. "He was a light-red minister," or "She was a dark-red sister," etc.

Imagine what it would be like if Christians became "color-blind"... or better yet "crimson-sighted". Imagine what it would be like if we only saw the Blood of Jesus on another person who confesses Christ as his/her Savior.

Instead of "black" churches or "white" churches or even "mixed" churches, we would just have **the church**. We could identify each other, perhaps, as "light-red" or "dark-red" for personal identification purposes, such as "Just go to that dark-red usher over there and he will direct you to the bathroom." However, we would really not see color...we would just see Christ in each other!

Wow! What a concept! Do you think maybe the Lord Jesus actually meant for us to be in **unity**? I personally think He did. However, there are other lessons that Christians and non-Christians alike can learn from this "green" business.

Changing Perspective

Whether you are a Christian or not, the simple strategy practiced by the Marine Corps illustrates the principle I just mentioned: If we can change our **perspective** (or how we view other people), then we will change our **behavior** toward them in the process. We have to grow away from identifying ourselves primarily by ethnic labels or color variations, and begin to identify with what we have in common with one another. Are we all Americans? That is a good place to start if we want to see change in our country to abolish the lingering affects of racism and bigotry still affecting our society.

Perhaps if we could just focus our personal identification on the **American** part of our label (African Americans, Latino Americans, Jewish Americans, Caucasian Americans, etc...) we could find the common ground necessary to end the ignorance of one another, and begin the work to break down the barriers that have kept the different races apart in this great country. Then, and only then, can the real work of Civil Rights and racial equality be accomplished through us. Setting aside color, ethnicity, and even political differences, we could then perhaps agree on the changes necessary to see real reformation in our society.

Christians, on the other hand, have an even greater responsibility in this area: If we identify with Christ, then we should identify each other the same way. Is that other person you are talking with a believer? Then you should love him or her as your own brother like

Jesus commanded you to in John Chapter Thirteen:

> *"A new commandment I give unto you, That ye love one another; as I have loved you, that ye also love one another. By this shall all men know that ye are my disciples, if ye have love one to another."*
>
> (John 13:34-35)

Historically, Christians have done a pitiful job at times obeying this command of Jesus, but things are changing. I believe that we are on the verge of a great awakening in the Church that will end much of the bickering, fighting and "denominationalism" that has hindered us from being the force of change God has destined us to be in this world. We are on the verge of a "love revival" that will cause the greatest revival ever seen in this country, and even the world, when we no longer see color or denomination as a hindrance for us to love each other! It will begin once the Body of Christ gets a firm grasp on the proper biblical interpretation and application of God's love, and then obeys His command to love each other as He has love us.

CHAPTER 11

White Man In A Black Man's... Church?

My wife and I had left our last pastorate in a small town in Ohio when we took a trip down to North Carolina to visit my mother and pray about what we were going to do next. On the way, we decided to take a route that would bring us through Richmond, Virginia, again so that perhaps we could spend a little time "catching up" with our pastor.

I had been ordained and sent out from my home church back in 1993 to pursue my call to ministry. We kept in contact off and on with my home church and pastor, but had lost touch with them during the preceding months of my departure from this pastorate. Feeling the necessity to inform him of our most recent events of ministry before heading to North Carolina to recharge and seek the Lord for new direction, we made a point to attend the second morning service so we would have an opportunity to meet with him for a few minutes before hitting the road.

He was delighted to see us when we came up in the greeting line after the second service, "Richard! What are y'all doing in town?" I told him we were on our way to North Carolina to see my mother and wanted to stop in for a service and to see him.

"When are you coming back through Richmond?" he asked. I was not sure of an exact day so he asked me to give him a call so that we could get together for dinner and all of us "catch up" with each other. After a few more pleasantries and hugs, we headed off down the road to see my mother.

Several days into praying for direction for our lives and ministry, the Lord seemed to put it on my heart to visit a congregation in Wilmington, North Carolina where a minister acquaintance (now a good friend) of mine pastored a church. I gave him a call to let him know we were coming and get directions to their building, and we arrived in time for their Wednesday night service.

The service was very good, and I hit it off well with this new pastor friend of mine. He is a "dark-red" brother and the church is a mixture of various "shades of red" believers, so we felt right at home. After the service, one of his leaders came over to introduce himself to us. During our conversation, he seemed to have been "hearing" some things from the Lord concerning us, and shortly excused himself to go and talk with his pastor.

"That brother is prophetic," I said to my wife. "He's picking up something about us, I can just tell." I noticed him walking back towards us a few moments later and he said, "I needed to go ask my pastor if I could share something with you both that I feel the Lord has put in my heart. He said it was alright, so do you mind if I share it with you?" Of course, I did not mind. I was earnestly seeking the Lord for direction in my life so I thought, "If you've got something from the Lord to give me, bring it on bubba!"

I love being a Christian and being able to hear from the Creator of the universe directly to get direction for my life in things big and small. A personal relationship with our heavenly Father is *supposed* to be two-way communication between a Father and His children, so any believer who does not hear from heaven in his heart and through the Word of God is missing out on his privileges as a believer. However, I have also learned to appreciate prophetic ministry because we can often have trouble hearing what God is saying to us with all the "noise" buzzing around in our minds. Churches and believers who reject this part of Christ's ministry gifts to the church as found in Ephesians 4:11 don't know how much they're really missing out on... and how much it has **hurt** them to reject Jesus' gifts.

"Sure, brother. Let me know what you believe God gave you concerning us and we'll take it before the Lord in prayer to discern His Will in the situation," I responded.

He went on to share several things with us that I knew were from the Lord. Leaving the church that night, the pastor and his family took us out to dinner at a local restaurant that was open late. We enjoyed the fellowship with the pastor and his wife, but the things this brother shared with me were still burning in my spirit. I could not wait to get back on the road and pray the two-hour drive back to my mother's house concerning these things.

On the road I prayed "in the Spirit" over all that had transpired that evening, and the Lord revealed to me through it all that He wanted me to go on staff as an Associate Pastor at my home church. I had thought of that briefly off and on in the midst of the dozens of other "good ideas" that had been floating around in my mind as to what to do next. However, the "good ideas" seemed to be louder and more noticeable than the "God idea" that was trying to get through all the interference for me to obey. It is for just such occasions as this that the prophetic ministry *really* comes in handy to help you sort out all the "fluff" and get down to the real thing God wants you to do.

My home church at that time was a 4,000-member, predominately "dark-red" congregation. In fact, almost all "dark" with precious little "light-red" brethren scattered in the congregation.

White Man...in a Black Man's World

My pastor and "hands-on" spiritual father is "black" by skin color ("dark-red" by my definition—I have another spiritual father who I've only briefly met, but whose television ministry was the backbone of my early Christian training in the Word of God, and who still influences me heavily today.) Those issues were never a problem with me, of course, but you do not just walk into a church and ask the pastor, "You need any Associate Pastors on staff around here?" Neither is it good sense to walk in and say, "God told me to join your staff." I believed I had heard from God, but I needed Him to work it all out if it was going to happen.

I shared these things with Donna, of course, and then spent the next few days praying over them to see what the Lord would have me do. Donna reminded me of Pastor's dinner invitation, and we felt like that was the next step. Calling his office and working the phone for a couple of days (he is not the easiest guy to get a hold of), we had a dinner appointment scheduled that next Friday night with Pastor and his wife.

When we all met for dinner that night, and had ordered our food and fellowshipped a while, he asked me what I had been up to in ministry during the time we had lost contact with each other. So, I spent thirty minutes or so just filling him in on things. Then he asked me what we were planning to do next, to which I replied, "We're not sure, right now. I am seeking the Lord about that and I am sure He will make it clear to us soon." Although I was pretty certain in my heart that I had already heard from God on the subject, it was possible we were way off track and missing it. Therefore, I thought it best not to mention anything about my home church, but to wait for the Lord to confirm His Will through Pastor before indicating anything that would suggest I knew what God wanted me to do.

"Well, I'll tell you what's in my heart...," Pastor began suddenly, "You know, ever since we started this church, I have always had a vision that we would have people coming to it from all denominational backgrounds, and they have. I have also had a vision that we would have people of all different races coming to our church, which we have had to some degree, but not near as much as I would like. But, one thing that we have never had is a **Caucasian person** as an **Associate Pastor**. Not that we've ever discouraged it before, but there has never been anyone 'raised up' through this ministry that would be *qualified* to be put on staff as a minister, who happened to be white. You are a son in the ministry to me, so I believe you should be that first white Associate Pastor of our church. And who knows? Perhaps that will help other Caucasian people cross the racial barrier and come over to our church so that some of them could one day be ministers on staff here. Pray about it, and give me an answer by tomorrow night, because we happen to have an ordination service scheduled for this Sunday, and I would like to install you as an Associate Pastor of this church. If it's God, you should already have an 'inkling' of it in your spirit, so you should be able to give me an answer by tomorrow night."

We were stunned! God's confirmation of what He had spoken to my heart, and through that brother back in Wilmington, was far more dramatic and sudden than what we had anticipated! I had not mentioned *anything* about my home church up until that moment. In fact, we had only discussed our experiences in Ohio up until then. Then, whoosh! Out of the blue, he asks me to join the pastoral staff of my home church!

Pray about it? I could have given him an answer right then! I wanted to scream and run around the table a few times. However, just to avoid seeming hasty, I responded, "Okay, Pastor. We'll pray about it tonight and I will let you know tomorrow." I sounded so cool and calm on the outside, but on the inside I was screaming, "Oh, my God! An Associate Pastor of a 4,000-member church! Oh, my God!" In order to understand my astonishment, you have to realize that the Lord had been developing me as a minister off in the "back woods" of America in small towns and small churches up until then. The biggest one I had ever ministered in up until then probably only had seventy-five people in it. A jump up to 4,000 was quite a shock to our system!

Donna was in even worse shape than I was. When I excused myself to go to the restroom, she followed me there, and almost went in after me! She told me "There was no way I was going to sit there with them by myself!" She was still awestruck by their rank and position, while we were both amazed at what God had just done. Needless to say, I told him the next night that we seemed "pretty sure" the Lord wanted me to join the pastoral staff. All that needed to occur now was my "installation" into that office, since I had already been ordained by him several years before.

The next night on Sunday, there was a special ordination service, and a surprise for everybody who attended. After introducing and calling forward by name the other men he was planning to install that evening as Associate Pastors, he began his introduction of me last as one of the new Associates without telling them who it was. After several complimentary descriptions, he said "I know many of you don't know this brother because he's been away in ministry in other states for a few years. But, I want you to *trust me* in choosing him as an Associate Pastor, 'cause the brother is anointed. The last new Associate Pastor we are installing tonight is Reverend Richard Vermillion!" And with that I stood up (I had been seated on the front row, but most people until then just thought I was a guest). You could hear the gasps of shock, followed by a moment of silence, and then delightful surprise as applause began to spread through the congregation.

The people were pleased at God's selection of new Associate Pastors, including the "light, bright, and *really* white" one that stood up last. They had been properly trained from the Scriptures that race and color was no longer an issue once a person has come to Christ, and so the joyful response to the surprise of seeing their first Caucasian leader was an extension of the love of God in their hearts—and proper biblical understanding in their ***heads***. I was equally well received by my "dark-red" brethren there when I first ministered in the pulpit of that church about a year later one Sunday morning service, and the many times thereafter. God continued to bond our hearts together in the love He always intended us to live by, during my time ministering among the people of that church. I served the Lord through serving that pastor and church for four years before the Lord led me to move on to other things as I am doing now.

God's providence had trained me all my life, from one situation to another, teaching me things concerning ethnic issues in preparation for the ministry He had called me to. From the lessons on bigotry and racism learned as a adolescent, to instruction in the color "green" taught me by the Marine Corps, and especially through the Scriptures which caused it all to truly make sense, God had been preparing me for my future. Even today, as I write this book, God is ***still*** teaching me how to love and serve my fellow man and brethren in Christ—no matter what their skin tone.

Endnotes

Chapter 2 – Culture Shock

[1] Back Cover: *Uncle Tom's Cabin,* by Harriet Beecher Stowe Oxford University Press: 1998, ISBN 0-19-282787-1

[2] Although Apartheid-like situations can be found around the world, there are some here in America (primarily those of Native American ancestry—including a few ministers I know of) which believe that much of our Native American population today are under a form of Apartheid themselves since many tribes have been isolated off onto Indian reservations for years.

Chapter 7 – Bridging The "Sensitivity Divide"

[1] "Racism," *Microsoft® Encarta® 98 Encyclopedia.* © 1993-1997 Microsoft Corporation. All rights reserved.

Chapter 8 – Political Racism

[1] "Segregation in the United States," *Microsoft® Encarta® 98 Encyclopedia.* © 1993-1997 Microsoft Corporation. All rights reserved.

[2] "Racism," *Microsoft® Encarta® 98 Encyclopedia.* © 1993-1997 Microsoft Corporation. All rights reserved.

Chapter 9 – Teaching Mike?

[1] To get more information on Valerie G. Lowe's article *The History America Chose to Forget,* you can visit **http://www.charismamag.com.** Simply do a keyword search on "lynching" and you will easily find more information about this article and how to obtain a copy.

Bibliography

Charisma & Christian Life, "The History America Chose to Forget" by Valerie G. Lowe. November 2000 issue.

Microsoft® Encarta® 98 Encyclopedia. © 1993-1997 Microsoft Corporation. All rights reserved.

Uncle Tom's Cabin, by Harriet Beecher Stowe. Oxford University Press: 1998. ISBN 0-19-282787-1

Printed in the United States
903400002B